fav

11/19

Books should be returned or renewed by the last
date above. Renew by phone **03000 41 31 31** or
online *www.kent.gov.uk/libs*

Libraries Registration & Archives

 CSE
 CUSTOMER SERVICE EXCELLENCE
 Kent County Council kent.gov.uk

First published in Great Britain 2019 by Trigger

Trigger is a trading style of Shaw Callaghan Ltd & Shaw Callaghan 23 USA, INC.

The Foundation Centre

Navigation House, 48 Millgate, Newark

Nottinghamshire NG24 4TS UK

www.triggerpublishing.com

Copyright © Tova Feinman 2019

British Library Cataloguing in Publication Data

A CIP catalogue record for this book is available upon request
from the British Library

ISBN: 978-1-78956-041-1

This book is also available in the following e-Book and Audio formats:

MOBI: 978-1-78956-044-2
EPUB: 978-1-78956-042-8

Tova Feinman has asserted her right under the Copyright,
Design and Patents Act 1988 to be identified as the author of this work

Cover design Aimee Coveney at Bookollective

Typeset by Fusion Graphic Design Ltd

Printed and bound in Great Britain by Clays Ltd, Elcograf S.p.A

Paper from responsible sources

www.triggerpublishing.com

***Thank you for purchasing this book.
You are making an incredible difference.***

Proceeds from all Trigger books go directly to
The Shaw Mind Foundation, a global charity that focuses
entirely on mental health. To find out more about
The Shaw Mind Foundation visit,
www.shawmindfoundation.org

MISSION STATEMENT

*Our goal is to make help and support available for every
single person in society, from all walks of life.
We will never stop offering hope. These are our promises.*

Trigger and The Shaw Mind Foundation

A NOTE FROM THE SERIES EDITOR

The Inspirational range from Trigger brings you genuine stories about our authors' experiences with mental health problems.

Some of the stories in our Inspirational range will move you to tears. Some will make you laugh. Some will make you feel angry, or surprised, or uplifted. Hopefully they will all change the way you see mental health problems.

These are stories we can all relate to and engage with. Stories of people experiencing mental health difficulties and finding their own ways to overcome them with dignity, humour, perseverance and spirit.

Being a parent is hard enough in a world that demands nothing less than perfect; doing so with a mental illness is unimaginable. Writing with courage and bravery, Tova takes us through the highs and lows of parenting, exploring the enduring love between a mother and her child.

This is our Inspirational range. These are our stories. We hope you enjoy them. And most of all, we hope that they will educate and inspire you. That's what this range is all about.

Lauren Callaghan,
Co-founder and Lead Consultant Psychologist at Trigger

*To my daughter Katie, who with openness and courage,
gave me permission to write about our family's journey.
Thank you for encouraging me and sharing your
ideas to birth this project.*

Disclaimer: Some names and identifying details have been changed to protect the privacy of individuals.

Trigger encourages diversity and different viewpoints, and is dedicated to telling genuine stories of people's experiences of mental health issues. However, all views, thoughts, and opinions expressed in this book are the author's own, and are not necessarily representative of Trigger as an organisation.

INTRODUCTION

My daughter's name is Katie and right now, she's 28 years old. However, if I close my eyes, I can see her as snapshots through time. Small ordinary moments that dot the narrative of our complexly woven lives.

She's a newborn bundle of promise swaddled in a white blanket with pink kittens. She's a five-year-old licking the bottom of a dripping ice cream cone while giving me the inside scoop of kindergarten intrigue. She's a ten-year-old who goes to bed early on Sunday nights so she can listen to the weekly opera broadcast. She's a newly blinded 15-year-old who dresses up in a homemade sheep costume for a party and sheds cotton balls wherever she walks.

Katie is all these things but she's something else as well. She's a woman who grew up under the shadow of her mother's mental illness.

People with mental illness parent. That much is a fact. Amongst family members, friends, mental health professionals, teachers, and other parents, there are plenty of opinions about us and the way we parent. Everyone has their own bias. Every thoughtless comment can wound and every word of encouragement nourishes.

We aren't just parenting. We are fighting a war against our own minds at the very same time. We are brave and we are flawed.

We hope and we despair in equal measure. Most importantly, we love our children fiercely even as we fight our own demons.

I'll Be Right Back is the story of my mother love. From my very first tear of post-partum depression to the tears of joy I shed as my child crossed the threshold into adulthood, it chronicles the experiences of Katie and me as a family. A special family that loves deeply, laughs joyfully, and suffers greatly, all shaded by mental illness. I share our story, with Katie's approval, because parents with mental illness and their children need to know that there are others like them out in the world fighting the good fight.

CHAPTER 1

A NEW BABY

She had wet black kinky curly hair, onyx eyes, a ruddy complexion, and a perfectly symmetrical head only a C-section baby is blessed with. Swaddled in a white blanket with pink kittens, she couldn't have been more perfect if G-d had molded her in heaven and angels had handed her to me personally.

28 hours of a Pitocin-induced labor and an emergency C-section had left me physically and psychically spent. Yet, here she was, wiggling, mewling, and probably wondering what the heck just happened to her.

Aren't I supposed to be the source of all her answers now? Isn't this what parenting is? To be there for your child completely? I pondered the terrifying responsibility I now had as I watched her shove her tiny balled fist into her toothless mouth. "G-d, help me, please," I pleaded out loud. A nurse looked at me bemused.

She needed a name. So I gave her one: Katie. The nurse in the room kept trying to extract birth certificate information out of me and all I could do was vomit from all the medications I had been administered. Joe, my husband, was going to have to fill in the details, I told her. I had my head in a plastic pan. *Where is Joe?* Last I saw him, he was asleep in a chair and the nurses were trying to rouse him. "Joe, Joe," they cajoled while shaking him. "You're about to become a father." The news was received with a sliver of an open eyelid. In the meantime, I was whisked down to an operating room with a trail of nurses, technicians, and obstetricians following in hot pursuit. *I guess Joe will catch up eventually. Maybe before the baby goes to college?* He did manage to arrive just in time to hear Katie's first cries.

Once I was settled back in my room and Katie was tucked away in the nursery, an unbidden tear streaked my cheek. I wish I could say it was a tear of exuberance and joy, but they were just tears, coming from somewhere. I certainly didn't know from where.

Hours passed. Joe made a quick appearance in my room but left, exasperated by my weeping. My hospital gown absorbed the torrent and the lactation coach showed up at 5am with Katie's isolet. She instructed me on how to hold my daughter for nursing. As I sat there watching, I couldn't help thinking, *I'm someone's mommy now?* The title struck me as unearned.

The lactation coach must have had some military boot camp experience. She ordered me, "No, you are holding her wrong, she won't latch on. Didn't you watch the video the hospital sent you before your due date?" *Video? What video? Did Joe forget to open the mail that day?* Tears were now streaming freely down my face and I confessed to my Nurse Ratchet clone that I didn't even know there was a video. Peeved, she curtly replied, "Then how do you expect to feed your daughter?" The thought of baby Katie starving to death because I hadn't watched a video turned my tears into a flood. I could barely catch my breath. Nurse Ratchet positioned Katie, she hungrily latched on, sated herself, and I cried hysterically because I hadn't watched a video.

Joe sauntered into my room that afternoon only to find me inconsolable yet again. Silently, he turned around and walked out, leaving me alone with my unbridled emotions.

That's how the 96-hour non-stop cry jag began ... over a lost video. I wailed through every feeding, every exam, every meal, and every well-wisher. I didn't know why I was crying beyond the fact that I hadn't watched this one video and my baby was going to starve as a result. I had no control over my own emotional process. My bed had to have been sunk in a lake of salt water by now.

Along with the tears came the shame. My friend, Ann, annoyed, demanded, "What's wrong with you? Your baby girl is perfect. Think how lucky you are."

I tried to swallow the river of tears but I only choked on them. They were coming down no matter how perfect Katie was or how disapproving Ann was.

So, instead of swallowing the tears, I swallowed my shame in their place. People stopped visiting. My obstetrician kept me in the hospital for over a week. Something that was pretty unheard of in 1990 for a complication-free C-section. Joe was cornered by my obstetrician. He was informed that the staff didn't know what to do with me. Dr. H said he couldn't release me while I persistently wept. But he also couldn't find anything wrong with me. Their solution was to move me from the obstetrical unit to a new hospital unit under construction. I guess they feared I'd disturb the other new moms if they didn't move me.

Six days after I gave birth to Katie, I was hidden away.

Perfect, the humiliation and banishment will really dry me out. But still I wept. After 10 days of no improvement, Joe, frustrated with me, told me my obstetrician had decided I needed to be sent home, regardless. I was shrugged off by the medical staff and deemed to be Joe's problem.

And so the beginning of the end of my marriage and my sanity was set in motion.

*

I sat in my wheelchair at the edge of the hospital roundabout waiting for Joe to wind his way through the circle in our new model blue Chevy Nova. A nurse was holding Katie's car seat / baby carrier. I studied slumbering Katie like she was a new piece of lab equipment I had to learn to operate. *She sleeps a lot*, I observed. *What happens when she stops sleeping?* I could feel the panic swell in my gut.

That moment, Joe pulled up alongside us. He exited the car, took Katie from the nurse and thanked her. As he tried to figure out how to buckle in this state-of-the-art contraption that was holding our daughter, I turned to my immediate problem. *How am I going to get out of this wheelchair without ripping out all my stitches?* I waited for Joe to turn to me and help. Instead, he returned to the driver's seat and waited for me to get into the front passenger side by myself. I couldn't move. Wracked with pain and shame, I turned to the nurse and whispered, "I don't know how to stand up." She smiled, gave me her arm, and with a death grip on her, I rose to my feet slowly. I could see Joe in the car, drumming his fingers on the steering wheel impatiently. I turned to my rescuer and thanked her, more tears forcing their way out. She gently touched my shoulder and whispered, "It'll work out, Tova." She opened the car door for me and gave me a spontaneous hug. *Isn't this supposed to be my husband's job?*

It was a silent car ride home to our newly purchased old Victorian home in our urban neighborhood. The house had so much potential but needed work. Joe fell in love with it immediately. Me, not so much. It was a go-along-to-get-along purchase.

As we approached the yellow-bricked three-story structure, I felt lifeless. Joe fumed in the car. Katie napped. *Is this what happy family life is?* As we pulled in front of our home, I saw a large pink oblong-shaped package sitting on our front porch. I turned to Joe. "What's that?"

"Who knows, maybe your coworkers sent something," he said, with a grunt.

I was curious enough about the pink package to shut off my tears for a moment. Joe went to Katie's door, removed all the child restraints, and carried her to our front door. As he fumbled with his keys, I had the sickening realization that I was stuck. I couldn't get out of the car without Joe's help and he didn't seem inclined to give me any. He looked back at the car and watched, annoyed, while I struggled to get out of the car unaided. Doubled over and panting in pain, I made my way to our front door and the curious package.

My obstetrician had given me strict instructions to not carry anything heavier than 10 pounds. I wanted to point out to him he was sending me home with a 10lb 4oz baby. How exactly was that math going to work?

I couldn't lift the package. I couldn't straighten up. I started sniffling, the tears returning. Joe slammed the door on me as I stood outside puzzling out what to do with the package. I looked at our front door and its braided pink and blue flower wreath wondering, *Is this even my home anymore?*

The package, wrapped in pink teddy bear paper, turned out to be from our friends Melanie and Darrel. Darrel and I had carpooled to work for years. He was an engineer at our Fortune 500 company and I was a new scientist hire in the environmental chemistry division. I didn't drive at the time and Darrel and I were matched in a carpool exchange. He was a young African-American man, happily married, two children, with a wicked sense of humor. We hit it off instantly. It wasn't long before Darrel invited Joe, then only my boyfriend, and me over to his home for a Saturday evening meal. Darrel's wife Melanie was the minister of an Anglican church congregation. As an African-American woman clergy, she was a groundbreaker. Yet even though I was Jewish, she welcomed me into their home as if I had always been part of their family. The four of us bonded that night over quiche, white wine, and a fruit and yogurt parfait. Our friendship grew as Joe and I began taking on the responsibilities of adult life.

Darrel and Melanie were true blessings in my life. Finding their pink package on my very dark day was more than a gift. It was a miracle.

Hunched over, I opened the door and gingerly stepped into our living room. Joe, not even looking at me, told me to put the package down over by the smoked glass coffee table. I stammered, "Joe, I can't lift it. I'm sorry."

"I've got to carry the baby and you too," he muttered.

I stood there, humiliated.

He returned with the package and dropped it on the coffee table. My curiosity got the best of my misery and I asked him if he minded that I open it. From the kitchen, he angrily hollered, "I don't care what you do. Just don't cry while you're doing it." I held my incision and tried not to heave. *At least if he punched me, I'd have a bruise to justify the pain.*

I turned back to the pink bundle and ripped open the paper. It was a pink baby bathtub filled with baby washing and changing supplies. It contained a note addressed to me: *Tova, call me as soon as you open this gift. M.*

I yelled into the kitchen, "The package is from Melanie and Darrel. Her note says she wants me to call her."

"Good," he scorned. "You can blubber on her too."

Ignoring his words, I called Melanie. "Hey Mel, it's Tova. Thank you so much for the gift. She'll be the cleanest baby in the neighborhood." I said with fake cheer.

"You sound awful," she said, and I could feel her concern through the phone. Immediately, at the sound of her voice, I began to, as Joe said, "blubber". "You sound like you could use a friend."

I sucked it up, determined to be strong, and tried to fake a laugh. "No, I'm okay. Joe and I are just tired. Katie is sleeping in her cradle down here in the living room."

"I can come over," she said.

I remained firm. "I'm going to take a nap. I have to sleep on the first floor because I can't climb the stairs too often."

"Has Katie had a bath today?" Melanie asked.

I answered in an undertone, "Yes, at the hospital. The nurse bathed her. I wasn't feeling well enough to get the bathing lesson though."

"I'll be over tomorrow morning at 10am. I'll help you set up the downstairs so you can care for Katie and show you how to bathe her."

I was awash in relief. "I'd be so grateful. I'm totally lost and Joe is overwhelmed," I said, almost gushing with anticipation that someone might be able to help, that I wasn't going to be alone in this.

"I'll bring breakfast too. All you have to do is boil water for tea."

"It's a deal," I said.

Normal new mothers have mothers of their own to call and analyze every aspect of bringing a new baby home. I wasn't a normal new mother. I had no one to call, not even Joe's mother, who'd had a stroke a year earlier.

I was the survivor of severe and prolonged childhood trauma. It was the reason I had no mother to rely on and the reason motherhood was completely unnatural for me. I had no clue how to bond with tiny Katie because no one had ever shown me how. I was emotionally fragile and childbirth exposed the underbelly of my weakness. My one asset was my intelligence. I could learn anything in the fraction of the time it took most people to acquire a task. If Melanie would be willing to teach me, I had hope Katie would survive under my care. Melanie could teach me how to bathe, diaper, and physically care for Katie, but she'd never be able to teach me not to be afraid of her or how to feel like her mommy. I needed way more help than baby bathing lessons. But no one in my life had any idea just how debilitated I really was and I had no voice to speak that truth.

*

Katie was rousing from her *Sleeping Beauty*-length nap. I heard her whimper then wail from the cradle. I tentatively made my way over to the handmade cherry wood cradle she had been sleeping in. The cradle was twice as big as she was. Joe and I had so much fun hunting for the perfect cradle. We went into every baby furniture shop, every handmade furniture boutique, and every custom wood shop we could locate in a 100-mile radius of our home. We found this cradle in a tucked away Amish boutique. We looked at each other and simultaneously squealed, "This is the one." I didn't know where that man had gone now.

Turning my thoughts back to my daughter, I guessed she was hungry. So, I bent over, picked up my crying child, and walked, still bent, to the couch where I could nurse her. It seemed I was a natural at this nursing thing after all, even without the video. *At least she won't starve. Take that, Nurse Ratchet.*

I turned on the television for a new episode of *Star Trek: The Next Generation*. As Katie enjoyed her meal, my first moment of calm in almost two weeks, I affectionately called to my husband up the stairs: "Honey, *Star Trek* is on and Katie's awake. We can have family time." We had a long-standing ritual of watching the program together before bed.

He growled from upstairs, "I'm busy."

I said nothing. *Maybe he just finds me repulsive now and can't stand to be around me.* My emotional wound deepened. As I burped Katie, I said to her, "Your daddy isn't coming." I had no idea how many times, in the course of her life, I would utter those same words to my daughter.

*

My one bright spot: Mel was coming in the morning.

I slept on the couch. At around 2am, Katie started to wail. As quickly as my stitched-up body would let me, I ran to her. *What if Joe hears her crying? He has to be at the hospital first thing in the morning. He won't tolerate Katie disturbing his sleep.* I picked her up. Shushed her. She continued to wail. I tried to feed her. She wasn't hungry. I checked her diaper. She wasn't wet. *Oh my, oh my. What do I do? I don't know what to do. Joe's going to be furious.* I walked the floor with Katie. Rubbed her back. Cooed to her. All while shaking in terror. Nothing worked.

Before long, Joe yelled from the stop of the stairs, "Can you keep her quiet?"

"No, I can't," I said, apologizing. I didn't know what else to do.

"Give her a pacifier!" he bellowed.

The pacifiers are in the nursery and I can't climb the steps. I groveled and confessed this to him. A few minutes later, a boxed pacifier bounced down the stairs at me. "Now you have one," he said, his words coated in derision.

I gave Katie the pacifier. It was magic. She sucked on it with great vigor and soothed herself back to sleep. *Note to self: always know where the pacifier is.*

I didn't sleep. Instead, I stared at the white stucco ceiling in our living room. An unbidden mantra pierced my ears.

I hate you

Daddy hates you

Die

The words spoke truth to me.

I rose, giving up on any kind of respite. I decided to make Joe a nice breakfast before he left for work. I heard our alarm clock beep and, as is his habit, Joe hit the snooze alarm. I made scrambled eggs with cheese, English muffins, and coffee for him.

The smell of the eggs made me run to the powder room and wretch. *Joe doesn't need to know this. No one does.* At the third slap of the snooze alarm I knew I had to wake him up. I called with a forced happiness in my voice, "Rise and shine, I have breakfast ready for you." I was faced with silence, then a curse word or two. I cringed. I had no emotional tolerance for swearing.

I stood there, waiting for him to come down. I felt five years old again waiting for the belt lashes. Joe dashed down the stairs, tie unknotted, shirt untucked, and his professionally laundered lab coat dragging behind him. I was smart enough to know that silence was my safest option at this moment. He turned to me with rage in his eyes and said, "If you had been a decent mother and kept Katie quiet, I wouldn't be late for the hospital." I stayed silent, handing him his coffee and he dashed out the door.

The second the door closed, I collapsed to the floor, curled into a ball, and piteously wailed a kind of pain that shredded my soul. I woke Katie up. Now mother and baby were howling in a pathetic duet.

The doorbell chimed. I looked at my watch. 10am. Mel, like me, is always punctual. I sat up on the floor and struggled to my feet. I didn't have time to go to the powder room and wash my face, brush my teeth, or braid my hair. Melanie would just have to take me as I was, dressed in two-day-old clothes, filthy, and with red swollen eyes. I painted on a smile and opened the door.

Before I even got a greeting out to her, she said, "Thank you for letting me come." She took my hand and I leaned my head on her shoulder. I said nothing. "When was the last time you had a shower?" she asked.

I confessed it had been before Katie.

"Well, before we bathe Katie, we have to make sure Katie's mom gets a shower." I told her the stairs were hard for me to climb and I had to keep the stitching dry. "Plastic wrap and my shoulder should do the trick," she said. She helped me up the stairs and poked around the nursery for useful items for Katie-care. She told me how to protect my incision with plastic wrap. I showered a long, hot, stinging, shower.

When I got out, I made my way to the kitchen, wet-headed but clean. Mel had laid out the perfect tea party, cranberry-orange scones and steaming mugs of English breakfast tea. I looked at all the food, reaching for a mug of tea, the warmth spreading into my fingers. All the while, Mel was studying me. I picked at a scone. She probed carefully, "How's Joe adjusting to fatherhood?"

I stared into my mug and a teardrop made a ripple on the surface of the steeped liquid. I felt bad for crying in front of her, wanted to appear strong, but I wasn't.

"That bad, huh?" she said.

I looked up at her pitifully and confessed, "He's so mean to me, Mel, he's so mean. I cry all the time and the more tears I weep, the crueler he gets. I need his help and he acts as if Katie isn't even here and I shouldn't be."

"Do you want Darrel to talk with him?" Mel asked. "You know he'd be honored to."

"And if Joe is mean to Darrel too? I couldn't bear that."

Melanie laughed. "Can you imagine Darrel being bothered by anything Joe might say?" She managed to get me to smile a little. "I'll ask him tonight. We'll leave this in the hands of the men. Right now, Katie needs to meet her yellow rubber duck."

Melanie was a wellspring of information. She was, after all, a mother of two. She knew how to make bathwater the perfect temperature; showed me how to support a slippery soaped up baby; showed me umbilical cord care; gave me at least 10 more reasons why newborns might cry; taught me about swaddling. She even set up the first floor so I could change and diaper Katie without climbing any stairs. Everything I needed from the nursery she brought down to me.

We had more tea as Katie slept peacefully. I couldn't speak except to thank her repeatedly and guiltily. "When is your maternity leave up?" she asked.

"Six weeks," I answered listlessly.

Delicately, she said, "That's a long time to be isolated and unsupported." She handed me a card. On it was printed in big letters "Warm Line" with a toll-free number. "Use this, 24 hours a day. There'll always be someone on the other end of the phone to listen and care. No matter how bad a day you're having or how mean Joe is."

"Mel, I feel like I can't do this. I don't even have a mother to rely on."

"You can rely on me, Tova. Darrel and I love you, Katie, and even Joe. You've been good friends to us. It's a privilege to return the favor."

*

A few days later, I noticed that Katie was particularly fussy since waking up from her afternoon nap. I tried all the tricks Mel had taught me and yet she still screamed. This wasn't her normal cry. I didn't know this cry. Although how would I know? I had only been a mom for a few weeks. Still, she didn't sound right. Something in me told me there was something wrong here.

I took off her receiving blanket to diaper her and she was on fire. I went into emergency mode. I'm not the panicky type in an emergency. I focus on resolving the crisis with cool reserve and then I'm a total mess after.

I took Katie's temperature: 102°F. As she screamed, I called Daniel, our pediatrician. Daniel worked with Joe at the hospital and it was natural that he'd become Katie's physician. I got his receptionist. I told her who I was and my situation. She sent my call straight back to Daniel. He told me fevers that high in newborns were rare and to take her to the Children's Hospital

Emergency Room immediately. I didn't know where Joe was, although I had tried to reach him at work. I called Mel. She said she'd track him down for me.

I called a cab because I was still on driving restriction and took Katie straight to the emergency room. The triage nurse grabbed her right away. Daniel had called ahead of us reaching the hospital and had made them aware of what was coming their way. The resident told me they were going to do a lumbar puncture to test for meningitis. I froze. I begged to stay with her. The resident said, "No, we don't allow parents in the procedure room." He turned and left.

Where is Joe?! I screamed in my head. I sat in the waiting room, desperate for news and desperate for my husband. Neither came along in a timely fashion.

Joe eventually appeared in the waiting area of the ER. I ran up to hug him but he kept his arms rigidly at his sides. I filled him in with what had happened. He looked at me, disinterested, and said, "I'd rather hear about it from the attending." We sat on opposite sides of the waiting area. I wasn't crying. In fact, I wasn't anything. My essence that had wept so piteously was now drained.

The attending called us in and said they were admitting Katie for a possible infection. I told him I wanted to stay with her. Joe took the attending aside and had one of those medical chats healthcare providers have with each other. A nurse came up to me and said very kindly that they were taking Katie to her room and I could follow. Katie had an IV and had stopped crying. I desperately wanted to hold her but had no idea if it was even allowed. I asked if I could nurse her. The nurse smiled and said I could.

When we got to her room, she had a roommate, a baby who'd had meningitis but was diagnosed too late. As the nursing team got Katie settled, I introduced myself to the young woman who I assumed was the baby's mother. Her face was completely blank. It's hard to know at that point whether conversation would help or hurt. I decided to let her make the next move. I nursed Katie and the staff took over from there. Truthfully, I don't remember the medical routine. All I knew was it would be days till the cultures came back and my job was to nurse her.

Joe joined us in the hospital room. We formulated a plan. I'd stay with Katie around the clock. He'd go to work and come to the hospital afterwards. He'd bring me food. Not that I could keep anything down at this point, but it was the first humane gesture he had made toward me since Katie's birth. I wasn't going to refuse.

*

It was past 11pm and Joe left for home. He never hugged me, reassured me, stroked Katie, or talked to Katie; he just left. I looked over at the tortured young woman. She couldn't have been more than 19 or 20. She was clearly alone in the world. The staff dimmed the lights. I stretched out in the recliner and quietly recited my bedtime prayers.

Without anything from me, the young woman began to speak. She told me her harrowing story in a monotone whisper. I didn't even know her name. I was there to bear witness to her horrendous suffering because no one else was there for her. And I didn't even know what to call her. In the dark, I jumped between prayers for her daughter, prayers for Katie, and listening to the young woman's gut-wrenching pain.

And all the while, I could hear that same mantra over and over again, Katie whispering in my ear, telling me how much she hated me, how much Joe hated me, how much I should kill myself. I tried not to let it worm at me but the constancy of it wore me down.

Katie stayed in the hospital till all the cultures came back. She had a urinary tract infection, nothing more serious than that. The unit nurses celebrated and detached Katie's IV and monitor. I was finally free to scoop up my daughter and feed her unencumbered. As I diapered, dressed, and bundled her, I looked over at the empty isolet in the far corner of the room. The young woman and her daughter had been discharged. She left never sharing her name. There was no expectation that the little girl would survive. The young woman wanted to take her daughter home anyway. No one told her she couldn't.

Mel picked us up from the hospital. I completely broke down in her car. I cried for the young woman, I cried for Katie's pain, and I cried because something deep inside me said tears were all I had left.

CHAPTER 2

A MOMMY LOST

"Good evening, welcome to the Warm Line. I'm Emily. What's your name?"

"I don't want to give you my name. I'm scared."

"I'd like to call you something. Do you have a name you like?"

"I'm Jewish. Shoshana is one of my favorite names."

"Hi, Shoshana."

"Hi, Emily."

Then the crying started, tears running down my face, onto the kitchen table, puddling under a placemat. The disembodied voice on the phone gently said, "I can hear you are in terrible pain, Shoshana. Maybe I can help."

Crestfallen, I whispered, "No one can help me."

Emily nudged, "But you called."

A half smile cracked my cheeks. "You got me there. I just don't know how to do this."

"Do what, Shoshana?"

After a pregnant pause, I said, "Talk."

"Tell me what got you to pick up the phone."

"I'm a new mom."

Emily was perky. "A boy baby or a girl baby?"

"A girl baby, Katie."

"How old is Katie?"

"She's five weeks old."

"Ah, a wee one," Emily said with a twinkle in her voice.

"She hates me."

The tenor of Emily's voice dropped and her cadence slowed. "What makes you think Katie hates you, Shoshana? You are loving enough to call when you needed help to be her mommy."

"Katie hates me because Joe hates me."

"Is Joe Katie's dad?"

I nodded and then realized Emily couldn't see me. "He's my husband but he doesn't want Katie or me anymore. Katie blames me. I blame me. I shouldn't exist. I'm not stupid. I'm a scientist and I have to go back to my lab next week. Joe's not stupid. He's a medical professional. But I'm garbage and Katie wants a different mommy and I should get her a better mommy."

I'm hysterical by this point, unable to even catch a breath because I'm crying so much. Emily lets me until she hears a break. "Does your obstetrician know any of this?"

"He won't take my calls because all I do is plead for them to make the tears stop."

Emily fishes for more. "Do you have a relationship with Katie's pediatrician?"

I sniffle, "I do."

"Do you think you could call and make an appointment to see him without Katie? Pediatricians are good with new moms."

"Katie has an appointment tomorrow with Daniel. What am I supposed to say to him?" I felt totally lost, and I knew no one was ever going to listen to me. No matter how hard I tried to get them to listen.

"Trust me, Shoshana, you won't have to say much. Just show up. He'll know what to do."

She extracted two promises out of me. One that I'd take Katie to see Daniel in the morning and the other was that I would call her the following evening. She gave me her direct line and she promised to be on the other end of the phone when I called. I thanked her with no energy and no enthusiasm. She probably thought I was an ungrateful wretch. I was sure that Emily found me repulsive as well.

*

Daniel's office was comforting in its familiarity. Becky, his office manager, sat behind the sliding glass window and waved to me as I got Katie settled in her baby carrier. "Hi, Tova," she chirped.

"Hey, Becky," I said listlessly.

We got the insurance information entered and I signed in. I sucked in my breath and asked apologetically, "Becky, does Daniel have time to talk to me after he sees Katie?"

With a smile, she said, "For you, he'll make time."

I gave her a grateful nod and carried Katie to a two-seated chair in the waiting room. Katie slept. I got lost in my own dark thoughts as the voices screamed at me incessantly. A nurse's voice jarred me out of the dark place I was wallowing in. "Dr. Wolmark is ready to see Katie. Follow me, please."

I sat in a nondescript exam room while the nurse weighed and measured Katie. She was screaming from being handled, unwrapped, and placed on a cold scale. I tried all of Mel's tricks and still Katie shrieked. I imagined all the other patients wondering what was wrong with a mother who couldn't soothe her own baby. I wallowed in shame.

I didn't see Daniel enter the room. My head was buried in my hands and I was repeating over and over again, "Katie, I'm so sorry. I'm so sorry. I'm a terrible mother for you. You deserve so much better."

Daniel greeted me with compassion. "Hi, Tova, and whatever could be wrong with Miss Katie?"

I responded in a whisper. "She didn't like being weighed."

He laughed and said, "It's my turn to make her unhappy."

After a thorough exam that Katie wailed through, Daniel pronounced her perfectly healthy and growing nicely. I looked at him, desperate. "I'm not starving her?" I asked. Daniel reassured me that my nursing was perfect and Katie was in no danger of starving. I burst into sobs and apologized to him over and over again. It seemed to me all I did now was weep and apologize. No wonder Joe hated me. Seeing the state I was in, Daniel asked me if we could talk. He asked the nurse to entertain Katie and he ushered me into his office.

I put my head on his desk and agony gushed out of me and all over Daniel's desk. "Talk to me, Tova," he said.

And it all came out. The 92-hour crying jag, Joe's cruelty, the endless stream of tears I had no control over, and my certainty that everyone would be better off without me. I dumped it all on Daniel's desk, never once looking at him.

When I was done, he said, "It's pretty clear that you're struggling with post-partum depression. It happens sometimes to new mothers and we aren't sure why yet. I'd like you to see a psychotherapist who will work with you to find relief. Have you ever been in therapy?"

"No," I answered, battered.

"It's hard work, but it's healing. This will get better, Tova. I promise."

I couldn't let myself believe him.

All I had to hang on to were Daniel's promise and some woman named Sue. Daniel took the extra step of calling in his referral. I could tell by his conversation with Sue that they worked together a lot. Daniel got me an appointment for the next day, which is pretty unheard of in the healthcare field. Sniffling, I thanked Daniel for being so proactive. As I got up to leave, he said, "I care about you. Call me any time and I'll be there for you." I thanked him, but I didn't believe him. Why would anyone care about me?

That evening, I called Emily, as promised. I told her about the psychotherapy appointment. Emily sounded audibly relieved. We hung up with conditional commitments for future calls if I needed them.

The next morning, I sat in my car outside a home on Lilac Court. *This is a psychotherapist's office?* I watched as a middle-aged woman quickly descended the patio brick front steps and ran to her car. She looked upset. *Does everyone leaving a therapist's office look upset?*

I realized it was my turn to ascend the brick stairs. Sue told me to just walk in when I arrived. I felt weird, invading someone's home like this. I stared at her front door for a moment and contemplated what I was about to do when the door suddenly opened. Standing in front of me was a statuesque woman with chestnut brown hair, green eyes, and a welcoming smile. *She's really pretty. I'm hideous. That's why my husband won't touch me.* I shook her hand limply and said, "I'm Tova. Dr. Daniel Wolmark sent me." She welcomed me and asked me to follow her to her basement office.

The office was dark. I didn't care though because it felt in line with my misery. I didn't know where to sit. As I hesitated, she offered me the couch or the overstuffed chair. I took the chair. As soon as I was enveloped in its cushions, the tears I promised I wouldn't show her flooded out.

She began softly. "Daniel says you have a five-week-old baby girl named Katie." I nodded without looking at her. "Where is Katie right now?" Looking at my hands, I told her my friend Melanie had her. "Melanie sounds like a good friend."

I whispered, "Melanie is the best. I work with her husband and she and I became friends. She's the only person I trust."

Sue prodded, "Not even your husband?"

I blurt out, "Joe finds me hideous. All I do is cry, apologize to Katie for being a worthless mom, and listen to her plead for another mommy."

"You mean Katie's crying means she's pleading?"

"No, her words do. Katie is smart. She speaks to me."

Sue paused for a moment. "Tova, newborn babies only communicate through crying."

I got defensive. "Katie speaks in full sentences to me." Sue asked me what Katie said. "She wants me to die. She's right. Joe will be a great father to her once I'm dead."

"Do you ever think about hurting Katie?"

Horrified, I screamed, "No, never! Katie is perfect! I'm the one who is defective!"

Sue tried to soothe me. "I had to ask, Tova."

I balled up as if I too were an infant and became entirely noncommutative. I began to feel hatred for this woman. *How is this discussion supposed to help me?*

As I lay there, Sue spoke very softly and very deliberately. "You have severe post-partum depression but we can work through it. I'd like to see you every day for a while and you can call me in the evenings if you need to talk."

I looked at her and I let out my deepest, darkest parenting secret. "I diaper Katie with my eyes closed. I can't bear to see how innocent and vulnerable she is. It makes me vomit."

Sue only nodded at my revelation and said, "We can work on this too." I suddenly started to like her a little bit better. She looked up at the clock and, almost with regret, said our hour was up. "I want to see you tomorrow, same time, and call me if you need to talk."

I left her office not really sure what I thought of therapy. I held her number in my hand, brightening at the thought that I was a little less alone.

My journey into mental health treatment had begun.

*

My driving restrictions lifted, I drove home realizing I had never mentioned to Sue that I had to return to work the next Monday.

Maybe going back to work would be good for me.

Joe and I picked out a babysitter for Katie. She was a vivacious 32-year-old woman, married, with a child development degree. I wondered if Katie would communicate to her or if she only did with me. *I'm sure Jill will tell me.* Sue's denial that Katie could talk drove me underground. Clearly, if I didn't want to be humiliated, I would have to keep this part of my relationship with Katie a secret.

As I pulled into our driveway, I had the dawning realization that I hadn't sobbed on my way home. Maybe there was something to this psychotherapy thing.

I decided to keep my appointment with Sue the following morning. There didn't seem to be any reason not to. As I walked through our front door, I heard Melanie talking to Katie and Katie wasn't wailing. A pang of profound embarrassment washed over me. *Why doesn't my daughter stop screaming for me?* But I wasn't jealous of Mel. I was in awe of whatever special skill she had that made my baby happy. I began, yet again, to feel the depth of my own worthlessness. The crying reprieve had ended.

*

"TOVA!" Joe yelled at me from the second floor later that evening. "DAVID'S ON THE PHONE!"

Surprised that my Lab Director would be calling me at home, I picked up the downstairs extension and hesitantly greeted him.

"Hi, Tova. I'm just calling in to be sure Monday is your return day. Data is piling up and boy do I need you!"

Being wanted was a feeling I hadn't felt in a while. "Yep. I'll be there Monday at 8am."

David teased, "We'll kick those vagrant project managers out of your office in no time. And we have a surprise for you."

"You mean a surprise like 1500 cyanide reports to analyze?"

David laughed and quipped, "Not cyanide data, mercury data."

"In that case, I'm going to need another six weeks of maternity leave to rest up."

"No," he said. "We just got you something special for your office. The staff is pretty jealous. I picked it out personally."

It was nice to know someone missed and wanted me, even if they wanted me to go through mounds of chemistry data. I wanted to reach through the phone and hug him. In the background, David could hear Katie fussing. "Ah, well, I guess motherhood calls. See you Monday, Tova. We're having donuts in your honor."

He hung up. I teared up. Not from the depression but because I was blessed with a really good director and a great job. I looked forward to Monday and my surprise.

Joe came down the stairs and nervously asked what David wanted. I replied with a smile, "To welcome me back. He misses me."

The worry on his face disappeared instantly and he sniggered, "At least someone does."

*

During my maternity leave, despite my depression, Katie and I had developed a kind of routine. In the morning, I'd bathe her, feed her, and talk to her. Mid-morning, I'd rock in the rocking chair in her nursery and sing to her. In the afternoon, I took her to the park and pushed her in the stroller around the circumference of the gardens. If she were older, I'd have put her in the baby swing and gently pushed her.

I was always on the look-out for bunnies. Even though Katie couldn't see the gentle creatures, I'd point them out to her and tell her stories about how much I loved the fluff balls. I told her about my neighbor when I was growing up and his hutch of rabbits, how I spent every afternoon after school holding baby bunnies and hand-feeding them. Those bunnies were the one gentle thing in my wretched childhood. Katie seemed interested and I was sure she'd grow up to appreciate the little critters as well, a rare bonding moment for mother and daughter.

I took good physical care of my daughter. Despite the tears, the depression, the suicidal thoughts, and Joe's contempt, Katie was always clean, fed, and properly dressed. What was missing between my precious newborn and me was emotional bonding. I was so afraid of her. So afraid of her innocence and vulnerability that I didn't dare connect for fear of hurting her. I didn't understand where this terror came from, but it was deep and had penetrated my heart. I had a long way to go as a mother.

Normal mothers bond.

I wasn't a normal mother.

People long ago had broken me.

CHAPTER 3

A MARRIAGE DISSOLVES

Even though my medical restrictions had been lifted and I was capable of driving, Darrel offered to drive me to work on my first day back from maternity leave and drop me off at Sue's after work. I gratefully accepted his kindness. En-route, we chatted about work, his kids, Mel's latest project at her church, and reminisced about some of our more humorous adventures while carpooling over the years.

Darrel was smart. He stayed clear of all emotionally charged topics. I think he wanted me to be in the best possible emotional space to return to work.

On the 25-minute commute to the lab, we never talked about Katie, Joe, my post-partum depression, or therapy.

I asked him, "Do you remember the day I got my license?"

He laughed. "Do I ever. I was sad to lose my copilot and a bit worried about the other drivers on the road."

He forced a smile out of me. "Yeah," I quipped, "the driving examiner for my road test was so afraid I'd give birth in his car. I swear that's the only reason he passed me." Darrel belly-laughed.

We arrived at security gate one and he gave me a thumbs-up. "You'll do great today," he said. I wished Joe had said those words to me as I walked out the door that morning. Instead, I'd eaten my bagel and he drank his coffee in icy silence.

I stopped at the security guard house to sign in and reactivate my badge. The security officer, whose name I couldn't remember, somehow remembered mine. "Welcome back, Tova. How's the baby?"

"She's wiggly and snuggly," I said.

He smiled at me fondly. "I remember mine at that age. Cherish these moments, they won't last for long." I smiled. "You are now officially back. I've reactivated your badge." I thanked him without much enthusiasm.

As I swiped through the security gate, I caught sight of a family of cottontail bunnies looking for a nibble first thing in the morning. I took it as a good omen that these gentle creatures were nibbling undisturbed. I wished I could pet them but intruding on their family time felt unfair to me. I teared up at the thought that Joe, Katie, and I had yet to have family time. Bunnies could manage what I couldn't.

I began to slip into the voices of my depression.

Then, from behind me, I heard, "Tova!" I turned around and it was David.

"Yep, I'm back," I said, trying to put my thoughts to the side.

"Thank goodness."

At least someone wants me.

I followed David into his office and took a seat. He frowned as he looked at me. "What's wrong?" he asked. I begged myself not to cry in front of him. We had a lot to catch up on and my depression was not on the menu.

We got through work topics, David bringing me up to date, and then we drifted into the personal. He asked how I was enjoying motherhood. When I looked at him, distraught, he reminded me that he had four children. "I get it."

It was like medicine to be talking once again to the person in my life I respected the most. David had hired me straight out of graduate school. Our rapport was instant. He was a brilliant environmental analytical chemist and he rose through the ranks of the environmental chemistry division of our company rapidly. As he rose, he gave me a hand up. I went from Assistant QA Director, to QA Director, to next in line to be regional QA Director. He knew he wanted me as his assistant but he was afraid I'd be too expensive. Little did he know I went from starving Peace Corps volunteer to starving grad student. The salary David offered seemed like a fortune to me. I jumped at his offer and a partnership, tinged with Monty Python quotes, was born.

"Okay, what's this surprise you have for me?" I asked with vague curiosity. "You moving my office to sample receiving?" I forced myself to make some jokes, to try to lighten the mood.

"Follow me," he teased, and we walked down to the first floor where my office was located. By my desk was the most enormous, comfy-looking, padded chair I had ever seen. David grinned at me, "It's your Captain Kirk chair." Sure enough, as I sat in it, all that was missing were the control panel buttons.

As I sat there, I thought about Joe's cruelty and David's thoughtfulness. A wave of pain caused me to shiver. "May we never again have any late-night data red alerts," I said.

"I'm leaving you to reems of cyanide data. Again, I'm so glad you're back," he said. I gave him a fake growl and he left me to my work and my desolation.

David's welcome was the high-water mark for the day. My thoughts kept drifting back to the serene bunnies nibbling unconcerned. *Why couldn't I have been born a bunny instead of a human being? Bunny moms are good moms. I'm wretched. Katie tells me that all the time and Joe screams it at me every day.* I wept even as I waded my way through cyanide, lead, and mercury data. I was on autopilot. I could do data review in my sleep. What

I couldn't do was soothe my baby or please my husband. *Please G-d, make me like a bunny mommy.*

Darrel picked me up at the security gate at the end of the day. "So, how was your first day back?"

"David's a gem. He made me feel almost human."

"Tova," Darrel said gently. "You are human, and a loving human at that."

No, Darrel, I'm a thing. Not a human.

I took the moment to ask Darrel about how his dinner with Joe had gone since Joe had said nothing about it. He sighed. "I can't tell you what we talked about, but I can tell you something is really wrong inside him. Please take good care of yourself and Katie because Joe isn't going to be any help."

It was a complete kick in the stomach to realize that Joe's cruelty was not a passing phase.

As we approached Sue's home, Darrel asked me how I was getting home. I almost asked him what home, but instead I said I planned to take a cab. "You don't have to. Mel's not expecting me till late and I have some shopping to do for her. I'll take you home after your appointment."

"Darrel, you've done enough."

He laughed and reminded me, "Driving you was my idea. You deserve a round trip."

"I wish you had a twin."

"Well, my brother is available, but Joe might not be best pleased about that."

"Darrel, Joe wishes I would just vanish."

Darrel took in a deep breath and gave me a compassionate look. *Darrel gets it.* I simply said, "Thank you for not dismissing me." I exited the car and climbed Sue's steps.

*

"I'm not human and I'm not a good mom like bunny moms," I confided to Sue. I curled up on her floor and shook.

Sue sat on the floor next to me, rubbed my back, and said, "Even bunny moms have bad days."

Answering as a child might, I said, "No, they don't." Sue asked about my diapering struggles. "I can't look at her. I can't. I'm always vomiting. She's so fragile, so vulnerable, so completely helpless. I can't witness it."

She nudged, "Tova, were you ever sexually abused?"

I curled back in my ball and in a wounded whisper squeaked out, "Uh huh."

A secret sneaked out from my past and into the present. I quickly ran from it. I told her my childhood was ruled by schizophrenics and my life was very different from other children's lives. Then I abandoned the subject, telling her I really didn't want to explore it with her. I switched topics completely and revealed what Darrel said about Joe. Sue was pondering something. "We'll get back to your abuse and your history at another time but only when you're ready. What you've shared does explain a lot about why you are struggling so much." Horrified, I realized I had shared far too much. Sue softly spoke, "That's enough for now. We have lots of sessions to talk about this."

Sue took the moment to tell me that she had received a call from Joe and he wanted her to see him professionally. "Can't he see another therapist? You're mine," I pleaded. She told me that by seeing both of us, she would be better able to help us with our marriage. *Or she'll take Joe's side and I'll be ganged up on.*

I didn't say this out loud. I was so scared to lose Sue. She knew I diapered Katie with my eyes closed. She knew about my sexual abuse. I feared my secrets, that I'd kept hidden for so long, were no longer safe. However, I had no choice but to trust her. *Maybe Sue's right. Maybe she can save my marriage.*

My depression was as deep and profound as ever. Katie's words stabbed me still. Cruelty oozed out of Joe, but Sue could save us. She said she could.

I wondered about confidentiality, but I chased the thought away. Sue had a plan to save Katie, Joe, and me. I felt hopeful.

*

Joe and I never talked about the fact that we shared a therapist. In fact, Joe and I no longer talked.

I tried to pin a timeline on when Joe's and my relationship began to crumble. I was always the submissive one to his dominance. I'd acquiesce and he'd demand. Even in our early days in Peace Corps, he was either showering me with affection or cruelly discarding me. On one hand, he'd tell me we were dating yet on the other hand, we could be on a five-hour bus ride and he'd never acknowledge I was even on the bus with him. I was then compelled to try that much harder to please him.

I guess our relationship was never equal. He was the first man I ever dated and I was so grateful he wanted me that I was willing to agree to anything. I lived for those moments when he tugged at me and learned to endure those times when he would neglect me.

After the rebuff, he always came back, except this time. He had become more neglectful and crueler but the kindness never returned. If it were just me, I'd live with it. However, we had Katie and it wasn't okay for him to do this to her. I knew we had a different relationship now because we had a child. A new pattern that was harming not just me but our baby daughter.

How was Sue going to fix this?

*

Katie was six months old and everything I did with her was tinged with fear and self-loathing.

Every night, I stared at the ceiling fan in my bedroom, consumed by ferocious memories of my childhood and the torments from my present. I whimpered, desperate for sleep, alone. Joe had moved to the guest room and it didn't seem like he was going to come back anytime soon. He didn't want to participate in any activities involving Katie or me. He had become just a roommate I passed in the kitchen and shared toothpaste with, nothing more, nothing less. I turned to Darrel and Mel more and more, letting them become my surrogate family.

At work, I buried my head into my crossed arms and wept in the privacy of my office. Only Sue knew the true depth of my torture. At the very least, I was still managing to get my work done. David hadn't noticed anything was amiss. However, he wanted me to do a data audit at one of the West Coast laboratories ahead of an EPA audit. My inspection would take a week. David was depending on me and he was the only person who saw me as being capable of life. I had four weeks to prepare.

However, as important as this was for my work, there were more important things to do at home.

Sue's plan to help our marriage clearly wasn't working and the voices I heard remained as loud and insistent as ever. I was still suicidal. It was all I could think about or talk about in therapy. The mantra and dark thoughts consumed me, blocking out everything from work to friendships. I isolated myself. I dove into my office and tackled whatever report or pile of data I had to address in complete seclusion. I was robotic with Katie. I cared for her needs but I couldn't feel any connection to her. I wanted to. I was desperate to. There was a canyon between me and my baby and I couldn't bridge it. That just made my mood all the darker. I had been seeing Sue for almost six months and nothing had changed for me.

I was desolate.

I decided to try a new strategy with Katie. I tried pretending to be a bunny mommy. I couldn't bring her dandelions to nibble on, but I could play with her more. I just didn't know how to do that. My hope was that Sue could teach me.

I sat with my feet curled up on Sue's rust plaid couch. It was kind of ugly and had supported its share of burdened bottoms over the years, but the overstuffed chair repulsed me for some reason. I think it was too close to the spot where I told her about my sexual abuse. I wanted distance from the ill-advised disclosure.

Sue was about to start our session, but I jumped in first. "Sue, can you teach me how to make Katie smile? She doesn't smile much and I know it's my fault."

"That's a great idea. Why don't you bring Katie to your next session and we'll see if we can get the two of you to bond better."

I sat in Sue's living room with Katie, waiting for my turn to descend into the basement. Katie was quietly sitting in her baby carrier exploring her new surroundings. Sue's dog, Sam, a Golden Retriever, poked his nose in Katie's carrier and licked her. Katie let out a squeal of delight that brought me spontaneous joy. I bent down to Sam and scratched her ears. She obliged by licking me too. I wondered if Joe would ever let us get a dog.

Sue snuck up behind me and caught our display of affection. "This is a great way to start, smiles all around." We descended into Sue's office. I almost asked if Sam could join us.

I extracted Katie from her carrier and bounced her on my knee. "See," Sue said. "You aren't terrible at this. I think with a little bit of coaching; you and Katie will do great." We propped her up in the corner of the ugly couch and Sue taught me the fine art of paddy cake, blowing raspberries, jingling keys, baby dancing, and, most importantly, smiling spontaneously. My lesson in baby play had my daughter clapping, giggling, and smiling. "See, Tova, you just brought your daughter an hour of joy."

"Thanks to you!" I said gratefully.

"No, thanks to your mother love. You didn't know how to start, but you're a natural. You're her mom."

I burst into tears, remembering how badly Katie wanted another mommy. The hour of play was over. Sue gave me an assignment: "Take 10 minutes out of every hour and play with her. Play will become more natural and Katie will smile more when she sees you. She can feel your mood. Counter it with play."

"I'll try."

"That's all I can ask," Sue replied.

*

Two more months, two long months, passed. Katie was eight months old. I did the play. I did my audit. David was satisfied with me. Joe was extremely dissatisfied with me. I was in a cycle. Tears, voices, self-hate, and faking competence with David became my life.

Then, out of the blue, Joe called my name, almost enthusiastically, when he returned from work. "What's up?" I responded warily.

"I just bought tickets to the Home and Garden Show. We can put Katie in her stroller and plan for improvements to the house."

My head was spinning. Eight months of neglect and verbal cruelty and now he was planning a big family trip and home improvements? *This must be Sue's doing.* I went along with his plan but I confess, I felt like a captive to his whim.

The Home and Garden Show was a cornucopia of house improvements. Everything from rubberized roofing to intricately latticed gazebos. Joe was like a little kid. The glass enclosed patio display and backyard fish pond model captivated him. I spent my time pushing a fussy Katie around in a stroller she didn't want to be in. I faked interest in Joe's house remodeling fantasies. Something seemed off. I couldn't put my finger on it, but something wasn't right with this whole scene.

When Joe had had his fill of fountains, exotic gardens, and granite kitchen counters, we mercifully left. I chided myself for thinking something was wrong. *You asked for family time. Well, you got family time.*

Why didn't it help? Why did I have a feeling of foreboding?

The answer came a week later. Joe called me into our living room and said he needed to speak to me. I thought it was about my illness or our marriage. Instead, his words were like an anvil dropped on my world. Staring at his hands, he whispered, "Tova, I'm addicted to prescription pain medication. I have been for years. It's gotten really bad since Katie. I was put on leave from the hospital last week. I thought the Home and Garden Show would make me feel better. It did. For a moment. Then I turned back to the drugs."

As he spoke, I covered my mouth, afraid the wrong words would escape. My first thought was, *How could he blindside me like this?*, but I said nothing. He chattered on about detox and rehab programs. An entire marriage of secrets, deceptions, and cruelty and I'm supposed to say what exactly? I uncovered my mouth and said, "Whatever you need, Joe, I'll support you."

It was a fake platitude because the truth was, I had no idea how I felt about him, his eight months of cruelty, and now this confession. It was clear I was expected to "be nice and compassionate" so I faked what was expected of me. Joe said, with his physician's help, they could get him into a quality program quickly.

There was a silver lining to Joe going off to eight weeks of detox and rehab. I'd be free of his cruelty for a time. I might get used to not being verbally assaulted on a daily basis. It was mean of me to think like this, but he had put me through hell. The switch from victim to caretaker was like whiplash. I would adjust, but it would take a paradigm shift in my already tortured brain.

Quickly didn't happen quickly enough, however. In the coming weeks, Joe was very open about displaying his addiction. I'd come home from work and he'd either be glassy-eyed staring at a daytime talk show or passed out on the couch. He suddenly became interested in being with Katie, but he was so drug-impaired that he was incapable.

One Sunday, I was in the living room vacuuming, Joe was holding Katie in the kitchen. I suddenly heard her scream and I darted into the room to find Katie on the floor. I shrieked at him, "What did you do to her?"

He slurred, "I dropped her."

Enraged, I shouted, "Don't you pick up my daughter again until you are clean and sober!" I scooped up Katie, soothed her, and carried her into the living room with me. Joe followed, pathetically apologizing repeatedly.

The bright side of this *Alice Through the Looking Glass* life was that he stopped being cruel. In an odd sort of way, he was now dependent on me for everything since he had no job and could barely brush his teeth. This sudden switch from being Joe's victim to his caretaker incensed me, although I kept my feelings to myself. Sue was so focused on taking care of him, the only conversations I was permitted about him were those of my unconditional support as a loving wife. I started hating Sue as well. So here I was, struggling with depression, hearing voices, fearing imminent harm, and I had to take care of the source of my misery.

I did the best that I could.

I struggled to manage Katie, Joe, work, finances, and house alone all while struggling with severe mental illness. I was drowning and Joe had denied me my only life raft. He asked me to not tell Mel and Darrel about his addiction and imminent rehab admission. I was lying to my closest friends on his behalf and they knew it.

The doctor finally called Joe with his detox and rehab assignment. They were expecting him the following morning. I helped him pack. I held him as he cried in fear of what was to come. I reached deep inside my soul and found a pool of compassion for him. It was just enough to keep me from doing to him what he had done to me for all those agonizing months.

As I drove him to the hospital, he said, "I love you, Tova, and I love Katie. I'll be a different man when I'm clean. I promise." Knowing very little about the psychology of addiction, I hung on the belief that he really meant his words. *Maybe without the drugs, there'll be a family for Katie.*

As we approached the imposing redbrick fortress that was the hospital, it occurred to me that it looked more like a prison than a hospital. I walked Joe in and we were greeted by an intake nurse. As we sat in her cramped, cluttered office, she asked me some questions and then gently told me Joe was in good hands and I could return to see him when Joe was ready to see me.

I was shocked. I was being dismissed. Apparently, I had served my function and she had no further use for me.

Joe stood up to hug and kiss me before I left.

He hadn't touched me since Katie was born.

Everything felt so surreal.

CHAPTER 4

EARTHQUAKE

I held my breath for eight weeks, agonizing over whether or not I still had a marriage and Katie still had a father.

I played out all the scenarios.

What would happen if Joe left? The abandonment would be crushing.

However, what would happen if Joe stayed? My stomach knotted up at the possibility that the traumas of the first eight months of Katie's life would continue in perpetuity.

As I watched Katie sleep, I wept for her. A mommy impaired by an illness she couldn't resolve and a daddy impaired by prescription pain medication. I whispered to her as the glow of her Winnie the Pooh night light cast a yellow halo around her crib. I swept a jet-black curl from her slumbering forehead. "You don't deserve any of this, Katie," I whispered to her. I sat in the rocking chair in her nursery and wept for my daughter.

The day of Joe's release from rehab cracked my veneer. I parked our car in a busy shopping district to pick up some baby items and some food I knew Joe enjoyed. When I returned to my car, a police officer was standing next to it writing me a ticket. "Hi officer, is there a problem?" I asked, trembling.

"Yes," he said authoritatively. "Your registration and inspection stickers expired three months ago. You can't drive this car."

I started to cry and blurted out my piteous story. "Joe, my husband always takes care of the cars. He's been in the hospital and we have a baby and I'm trying to work, care for a baby, and support my husband. Honestly, Officer, I've never renewed a registration or gotten a car inspected in my entire life. I've only had my license for nine months. If I don't have a car, how can I pick up my husband from the hospital? How can I pick my baby up from the babysitter? How can I get to work?" I stood on the sidewalk, a hysterical, sobbing mess. The inner conflicts of the past eight weeks played out on a busy city sidewalk in front of a police officer.

He softened his tone. "As soon as you have everyone safely where they need to be, don't drive the car till it's inspected and registered. I won't issue you a ticket this time."

I covered my mouth with my hand and whispered, "Thank you, Officer."

"I hope things improve for your family, ma'am," he said, before leaving.

I continued on to the hospital, completely rattled.

The hospital aide wheeled Joe to the discharge exit. I studied his face. Gone was the cocky man who wasn't afraid to tell the city's leading physicians that the medications they had ordered for their critically ill patients were the wrong doses. Now he looked hollowed out, tentative, and frail. As I looked at him, I remembered our wedding day. I remembered the hope. I remembered the love. In that moment, as I remembered what was and faced the unknown, I realized that I was no longer angry. I was being called upon to reach beyond my own pain and care for a broken soul. Marriage license or not, I had a higher calling. We drove to pick up Katie while he and I chatted about trivia. It was a weird kind of role reversal. Joe always drove if I was in the car.

Katie had a curious reaction to Joe's return. As he sat on our couch, smoking a cigarette, Katie would crawl up to him at lightning speed, stare at him as if she wanted him to pick her up, and scream if he did. He looked at me bemused. "What's wrong with her?" he asked, as if this was unusual behavior.

Annoyed, I said, "You've been gone for eight weeks and when you were here you treated her as if she wasn't. Give her time."

Joe grunted, "I screwed up, big time."

I almost snidely replied, "In more ways than one." Instead, I answered, "You can fix this. She's eight months old. You have time."

He looked at me with gratitude. "Thanks, Tova. I need her not to hate me."

It dawned on me. Joe, Katie, and I were having family time. It felt so much more real than the forced trip to the Home & Garden Show. I turned to him, took his hand, and said, "Welcome back, I've missed you." He couldn't look me in the eye.

That should have been a storm warning. The eye of the hurricane was passing over head.

*

I was expending every spare joule of energy tending to Joe and caring for Katie. Left unresolved were the screams that shattered my nights and the invisible forces that manipulated my days. My demons hounded me. They threatened me with harm. They cajoled me to suicide. My depression continued to envelope me. Yet, somehow, I held together. Was it love, obligation, or fear that was my glue? I don't know. It took only one final blow and I became unraveled. Several months after Joe's discharge, that blow came.

"We need to talk." Joe stood in the doorway of my bedroom and woke me late one night.

"Can it wait? David wants me at an engineer's meeting early tomorrow and I have to get Katie to Jill's at 6am."

Joe was insistent. "No, it can't wait."

The tone of his voice made me nauseous. "What is it?" I asked, terrified.

Still standing in the shadows, he icily muttered. "I want you and Katie to move out."

I was frozen in time. The words I had dreaded had just been spoken. All I could muster was a simple question. "Where are we supposed to go? This is our home."

Joe, a shrouded figure, answered flatly. "Just leave, Tova. *I don't care where you go*. I don't want you here anymore."

I heard him walk up the stairs to the third floor. I lay in bed, fixated on the rotating ceiling fan. I didn't cry. I wasn't in pain. I was vacant. My life's energy poured into a relationship that just dissolved. Despite the fact that I had a baby, no family, few friends, no home, and no marriage, I was completely calm. Where exactly were Katie and I supposed to go? My thoughts drifted back to Joe's words. I don't care where you go. I had to care. Katie needed me to care. I was all she had and she was all I had. What a cruel way to test if we had finally bonded.

I was desperate for a mom to call and commiserate with. I longed to hear an outraged voice and telling me he's not worthy of Katie and me. I didn't have that luxury though. I didn't have a mom of my own to turn to.

I went to the kitchen to make tea. It was 3am. Too early to wake Katie. Too late to beg Joe for a few more days.

I've spent a good portion of my life begging. Begging for the abuse to stop. Begging for help. Begging that the monsters go away. Was I now supposed to beg Joe to not make his infant daughter homeless for a few more days? No. Just like all the other abusers in my life, I'd give him what he wanted. I surrendered.

I spent the following weeks in a dissociative fog. It turned out I had more friends than I thought, people who were willing to help me out. Joe's relative took us in. Ann, a long-time friend of Joe's, reached out to me and found us an apartment. David gave me time off. Mel went with me to Joe's and helped me pack … everything. She made sure nothing Katie or I would need remained in the house.

The ultimate revenge was when I took the expensive bed Joe insisted we buy when I was pregnant. Joe didn't complain. Darrel sat with me when I had no words and no tears. I moved around the periphery of the swirling events in my life but didn't actually live them. I couldn't remember to eat, bathe, brush my hair, sleep, or even cry. Never once did Joe enquire if Katie and I were okay in this new life of ours.

Katie screamed whenever I was out of her sight. *How do I explain to her that Daddy told us to leave? How do I tell her that her daddy didn't love us enough to even care if we had a home?*

I asked Daniel, "What do I do now?"

He said, "Keep loving her. Keep getting help for yourself."

So I turned to Sue.

I continued to see Sue professionally throughout the upheaval. She was nurturing and a wellspring of practical advice. She made herself completely available to me any time I needed her, and I needed her a lot. Sue held me as I trembled and told me she loved me when I crouched on her floor empty and rocking. One evening, she called me and asked if I could use some furniture in my new apartment. She was buying a new living room set and wondered if I'd like her old set. I was thrilled. Mostly because I needed the furniture but also because she was offering me something tangible of herself. I would now be able to sit on Sue's couch, rock in her recliner, and put my teacup on her coffee table. Having tangible evidence of Sue's presence throughout my apartment would bring me a great deal of comfort. She told me that the furniture would be delivered Saturday and she would pay for the moving expenses.

As promised, the living room set was delivered and it fit perfectly in my apartment. I danced around the room, holding Katie. The furniture made me feel loved. I called Sue to thank her and let her know her furniture created a home when it had once been just an apartment.

She told me she was glad and then asked, "I'm having a few friends over for dinner on Sunday. Would you and Katie like to join us?"

I felt so special and so wanted. I accepted with a child's glee at being considered part of the in-crowd. What I didn't know in that moment was that accepting her dinner invitation would ultimately lead to my complete psychiatric collapse and leave Katie with no mommy and no daddy. Sometimes the most toxic poisons can taste so sweet going down.

We were part of many of Sue's dinners, holidays, birthdays, family gatherings, and vacations. Katie's third birthday party was an extravaganza. I took the day off from work and Sue joined me at my apartment. We hung pink and purple balloons, crepe paper, and streamers. I picked up Barbie party plates, napkins, and table clothes. I baked Katie a Barbie doll cake. The cake portion formed Barbie's dress and a Barbie doll had to be inserted inside the mound after baking. It was a delicate cake to make, but it was an act of love for me to bake it for Katie's third birthday. We ordered pizza and had cookies-and-cream ice cream. It was Ann's job to pick Katie up from day care and entertain her while all the guests gathered. We had a houseful: Sue, her husband, and their three children; Joe's mother and sister; Darrel, Mel, and their two children; Ann, her husband, and their twins; and Katie's friends from day care. We had a party filled with giggles, crushed cake, and Katie's new train set spread from the kitchen to the sunroom. A wild time was had by all. As the guests bid their regretful goodbyes and Katie crashed on the recliner, frosting stuck in her hair, I turned to Sue and said, "I love you."

Sue put her hands on my shoulders and replied, "I love you too, very much."

It was a good night.

One year later, I would be confined to a psychiatric hospital, being treated for a psychotic-manic episode. Katie's fourth birthday would go unnoticed. She would be a little girl lost.

*

My spiral downward after Katie's third birthday was rapid. It was fueled by unresolved bouts of severe depression, psychosis, and trauma memories so brutal, I often retreated into fantasy worlds to escape. I would close the door to my office, wedge myself into a corner, and rock silently for hours. I was reliving some of the most horrific moments of my childhood right there at work.

This time, David noticed something was off. He called me into his office and expressed his concerns. I told him I was doing my best. With a sigh, David replied, "I know you are."

At home, I would go through the motions of feeding and preparing Katie for bed. However, all I really wanted to do was rock on the floor with my stuffed bunny and crawl inside my mind for protection from the past. If Sue had been objective and clinical about my condition, she would have realized that her treatment wasn't working and was in fact torturing me. She might have referred me for an immediate psychiatric evaluation. Instead, she chose to continue to manage my severe symptoms on her own using hypnotic regression and endless hours of talk therapy. Because this recipe was a complete failure and I continued to crumble before her eyes, she began to distance herself from me.

I can almost pinpoint the moment when our relationship began to sour. During therapy, I sat facing a wall in her office, hitting my head repeatedly on the plaster. Sue commanded me to stop and when I didn't respond she came up beside me and hissed, "Tova, stop!"

I shrieked, "No, please, no. Don't touch me! Don't! Please don't make me stop!"

She walked upstairs, giving up and leaving me in her office alone pounding my head.

Soon after that, the dinner invitations stopped coming. For the first time in three years, Katie and I weren't invited on the annual summer vacation. Sue became cold and distant. Therapy sessions changed radically. The warmth, closeness, and love were gone. I was bereft. She was my mommy, my family. Yes, I had been ripped in two because of the dual relationship and it needed to end, but what I wanted was for her to stay my mommy and me see another therapist. The final straw was when she told me, "No therapy with me, no mothering."

It was an impossible choice and as a result I became psychiatrically unmanageable. Finally, after it was too late to avoid ruin, Sue referred me to a psychiatrist.

My disintegration ripped the fabric of every relationship of value to me. David felt I was a disruption to the lab and too impaired to do my job. He placed me on disability leave. Ann distanced herself from me because my illness frightened her and she didn't want me around her children. Darrel and Melanie had just recently relocated to Virginia. We spoke intermittently on the phone but they had a brand-new life to build. It was time for me to let them go.

Joe had completely vanished from Katie's life. He didn't show up for her preschool activities, never spent time with her, and never even paid child support. He had simply disappeared. Katie was spending a lot of overnights at a family friend's because I was so incapacitated, I couldn't care for her. I was incapable of managing even basic things like laundry and food preparation. Katie and I ate out every night. I'd put her to bed as early as I could so I could curl up on the floor, stare into space, and rock all night. I never slept. I had stopped functioning.

On a spring afternoon in 1994, Sue and the new psychiatrist she had finally decided to refer me to had me admitted to Franklin Psychiatric Hospital. I was not allowed to say goodbye to Katie or prepare her for my absence. I was banished from my daughter's life and there was not enough inside me to fight back against the onslaught. I believed Sue's pronouncement that speaking to my child would harm her.

At the hospital the last functioning bits of my life were dismantled. I would emerge from the admission a hollowed out human being who would need to be completely remolded in order to rejoin life.

I was referred to the psychiatric hospital in another state for intensive treatment for trauma and bipolar 1 disorder with psychosis. I was about to enter the world of the chronically mentally ill. No one seemed to care that I was someone's mommy. In fact, I was the only parent she had any memory of.

Katie and I often refer to 1994 as the lost year. She has almost no memory of it and I lost complete contact with her. I was confined for most of the year to the hospital. Katie was bounced from family friend to family friend never really having a home to call her own.

On Katie's fourth birthday, I was languishing in the "special care unit" of the hospital. This unit was reserved to treat people suffering from psychotic episodes. I pleaded with the hospital staff to let me call my daughter. I crawled to the nurse's station, begging: "She'll think I forgot her day! She'll think I don't love her! She has no idea where I am! Maybe she thinks I'm never coming back! A phone call will fix all that, please!" The response was a flat "no".

The voices of my tormentors laughed at me. I screamed back, "Shut up. Just shut up. You don't own me." But they did. I ran straight into the cinderblock wall that framed my room, slid down it to the floor and shrieked, "Katie, I'm sorry! I'm so sorry! I love you. It's your birthday and I don't even know where you are!" I vomited all over myself and I heaved violent sobs. There was no comfort for me on Katie's fourth birthday. I was sickened by the thought that there was no comfort for Katie either.

As the grief enveloped me, reality ceased to exist. All that remained were the dark creatures that taunted me and darted in and out of the interdimensional portal I was sure existed. *Fight them and Katie will be safe.*

It was the only power I had left.

*

Antipsychotics and mood stabilizers freed me from the "special care unit". However, my treatment was by no means complete. I was in this hospital to get trauma treatment. Mania with psychosis got in the way. The trauma floor was a gilded cage. There was a television and comfortable couches in the lounge. A room I shared with another woman complete with a desk, dresser, and closet. I was free to wander around the unit. Unlike in the special care unit where I was confined to my room, I had some freedom on this unit. Best of all, there were phones and phones meant I could call Katie. I was given a tour by the senior social worker. She showed me the group therapy room, the music therapy room, the lunch room, the individual therapy rooms, and the library. I was a little stunned by how inviting the atmosphere was and how many therapies there were available. As I pondered the contrast between where I had been and where I was now, it was hard to believe it was the same hospital.

"Can I talk to you, Tova?" I looked at the tall brunette with confusion. I had no idea who she was.

She read my face and introduced herself. "I'm Kelly, your therapist."

I replied, "Ah, thank you for clearing up the mystery. Sure. I can talk."

I followed her into her comfortable office. She explained that she was my private inpatient therapist and we'd be meeting three times a week. She also said I had a psychiatrist assigned to me and I'd meet him later in the day. Then the bottom dropped out of the conversation. "I received a call from your outpatient therapist, Sue." My stomach knotted at the mention of her name. "She has decided that she will no longer see you as a client and she's also ending your personal relationship with her."

She stopped talking and let her words sink in.

I looked at Kelly with a stoic expression that revealed nothing about my anguish. It was as if I had had a limb severed with a machete but just couldn't scream. Kelly didn't get it. How could she? She had just told me that my mommy was throwing me away like garbage because, why, I didn't know.

I finally whispered, "Why?"

"Personal reasons," Kelly said. "We'll work on this. I'm sure you have many complicated feelings about your former therapist."

"Can I leave now?" I whispered.

"Are you okay?"

What was I supposed to say to that? *The woman who let me call her mommy, who accepted Mother's Day gifts from me, who let me hold her hand as she went for surgery has just cut all human ties with me, and you're asking if I'm okay?*

In that moment, I hated Kelly. I hated her cavalier attitude toward the earthquake she just created in my life. I hated that she actually thought I'd talk to her about Sue and me. I hated her therapeutic platitudes. I responded with a curt "no" and walked out of the room.

*

I was only supposed to be at Franklin Psychiatric Hospital for two months. The first weeks I spent recovering from psychosis and mania. The remainder of the time was supposed to be spent on trauma therapy. The nuclear bomb Kelly dropped on me ripped up my treatment plan. My psyche was shattered, reduced to jagged shards. I had lost my child, my job, my independence, and my mommy. I was now allowed to make regular calls to Katie but she was four. She wasn't going to tell me about her day, or if she was sad, afraid, lonely, or safe. No one was giving me real information about her other than she was in Joe's care and she was doing fine. "LIES," I screamed every time I hung up. I didn't even get an explanation of how she ended up in Joe's care. I knew nothing about my daughter's life.

In a different time, a universe away, I would have known everything about Katie. I'd be attuned to her moods, her fears, and her joys. Now no one would tell me anything. The harder I pushed, the quicker people got off the phone and the more paranoid I got that I was being lied to. I was completely powerless to be any kind of a parent. So, I surrendered to that powerlessness and collapsed into a nonfunctioning heap. I balled up in a fetal position, unresponsive for long periods of time. I was uncooperative in groups, remaining sullenly silent. I'd sit in Kelly's office, staring at her, noncommunicative. I would barricade myself in my bathroom and refuse to go to groups. I didn't take my medications and my bipolar symptoms returned quickly. I was either wildly symptomatic with bipolar 1 disorder or a quivering traumatized mess. As a result, two months became eight months.

*

I didn't feel like a human being anymore when the psychiatric hospital released me in the fall of 1994. I was just one of the chronically mentally ill, devoid of hope. What could I possibly have left inside that was worthy of Katie?

I would have to answer that question somehow before I could be the mommy she needed.

CHAPTER 5

MOTHER AND CHILD REUNION

The Franklin Hospital staff would only release me if I had an intensive outpatient treatment program to attend.

Back in Chicago, I was admitted to a long-term partial hospital program. In 1994, partial hospital programs were places where the chronically mentally ill went to rot.

It was a weird arrangement. From 8am till 4pm, I was treated as if I was on an inpatient unit. It wasn't that much different from Franklin Hospital, just less gilded. But like magic, at 4:01pm, I was released to my own care until I was required to return the next morning and resume submission. From 4:01pm till 7:59am, I was suddenly supposed to know how to manage my life after a year of captivity.

I found a way to cope with the dissonance. I was on a first name basis with the pizza delivery boy. I watched endless hours of 1970s television reruns. I sat on my couch and dove inside the fantasies of my own creation. I was the heroine in the dramas that played out in my mind. I'd come to, realizing it was 2am and I hadn't moved from the couch. Forget laundry, bill paying, grocery shopping, brushing my teeth or showering. I'd take my medications, a hand full of pills, and curl up on my couch. Drifting in and out of a drug-induced stupor, I listened to voices telling me

THEY were coming. *Close the portal*, I'd scream in my sleep, but the portal was elusive. I could never quite locate it. I just knew it was lurking and delivering my tormentors. *How the hell do I close it?* I begged to no one.

At 9:30am, the Saturday after my first month back, my phone rang. It was Joe. "I have a meeting to go to, can you take Katie?" he asked.

I stammered, "I guess so, what time?"

"3pm," he said flatly.

"Uhm, okay, but she can't come here."

The house was barely habitable. We settled on meeting at Davis Park. I hadn't contacted Katie during the entire month I had been back. I was hiding from her. Dirty, disheveled, and way over-medicated, what exactly was I going to say to my five-year-old daughter who hadn't seen me since she was three?

I wasn't ready and yet I knew I had to be perfect for this reunion.

I tip-toed into the shower, oblivious to its temperature. Rummaging through my closet, I hunted for something that fit and was clean. *Brush your teeth*, I ordered myself. *You probably stink*. As unprepared as I was, a kind of excitement overtook me. *Katie, I'm going to spend time with Katie!* I had dreamed of this day for an entire year. *I can't blow this. Dear G-d please, I can't blow this*.

Joe pulled up behind me at the roundabout in the park. I could see Katie in her booster seat holding her long-time favorite stuffed animal, White Bunny. As Joe stepped out of his car, I took a deep breath, said a quick prayer, and greeted him. He was cordial. We spoke about the logistics of him picking her up and I inquired if she had eaten. It turned out she hadn't. *Ah*, I thought, *a mom thing I can do*. Feed her. I told Joe I'd take her to a local family restaurant when we were finished at the park and feed her. He could pick her up there. As he turned to leave, I called out, "I need her booster seat!"

He laughed, replying, "She's still in it. Give me a minute." That little exchange broke up the tension.

Katie opened the door of Joe's beat-up Chevy Nova. The same Chevy Nova that had transported her home from the hospital as a newborn. Joe and I named it "FAP" after the letters in the license plate. It was the car I learned to drive in and the car I occasionally hit a few mailboxes with along the way. I had an odd kind of affection for FAP. It reminded me of better times.

Stepping out of the car, Katie leaned into the door like she was hoping to melt into it. She did not greet me. She just stared at me, her Bambi eyes blinking from the glaze of the afternoon sun. I realized she didn't recognize me. Last she saw me, I was 130lbs and smartly dressed. Now I weighed 260lbs and I was in a sweatshirt and oversized jeans. She knew I was her mom, certainly Joe had told her that. However, her eyes told me she was searching for someone who didn't look like me. My heart broke for her. This was all of me I had to offer her, and it wasn't very much.

"Hi, Katie," I said cheerfully. She pulled on the trim of her sundress and brought it to her mouth. That was how she responded to my voice. I wanted to escape, but I stayed in the present. "Katie, did you know there are a lot of bunnies at this park?"

She let the trim of her sunflower dress drop and said, "I like the bunnies here."

Ah, an opening I can reach her through. "I love bunnies too and I know all their secret hiding places."

"Really?" she asked wide-eyed.

"Yep. I'm a bunny mommy."

She giggled. Joe stood next to the driver's side door and announced that he had to leave for his meeting. Katie turned to him, waved, and said "Bye, Daddy." Joe didn't respond to her.

He got into the car and made his way out of the park. Katie and I were alone, except for the flock of butterflies in my stomach.

Okay, now I had a real problem. I'd promised bunnies and I had better be darned sure I delivered on that promise. "Where do the bunnies live?" Katie asked quizzically.

"Well," I replied, "there's a patch of grass and dandelions at the end of that path over there where they like to snack. Want to take a peek?"

"Yes!" she squealed.

"Follow me, then." I offered her my hand but she didn't take up my offer. My heart wept. *Patience*, I said to myself. *This is the beginning of a long journey back for both of us.* I retrieved an old quilt out of my car trunk and walked side by side with Katie down the path and toward the clearing. She asked questions about bunnies: how many might we see; what colors might they be; could she pet them; could she feed them. I gave her gentle but realistic answers. I told her they were all wild bunnies so they would probably be brown and they'd be in a small group, most likely. Then I shared that bunnies are easily scared so they might not want her to go near them. I added, "But you can watch them, count them, pay attention to what they are eating, and watch them hop." She seemed satisfied with my answers.

As we approached the clearing, I scrunched my eyes tightly and begged G-d for there to be bunnies. I opened my eyes, and there in front of me were a family of rabbits, big and small, nibbling on dandelions. *If I ever doubt there's a G-d again, I'll remember this moment.*

I spread the quilt in a corner of the clearing so as to not scare the rabbits. Katie and I sat on the blanket and she counted bunnies. "Five," she said authoritatively.

"Yep," I answered. "Five brown bunnies."

She asked, "Do you think the little ones are babies?"

Now it was my turn to be the bunny authority. "Absolutely," I said. "I have no doubt the little ones are babies."

Katie leaned her head against my arm and I kissed the top of her silky shampooed hair. She didn't pull away. We named every bunny, several times over. We tried to decide which ones were the mommy and daddy bunny. She asked if she could try a dandelion. After all, if they were good enough for bunnies, they were good enough for her. I laughed and asked, "Are you hungry, Katie?"

"Kind of," she said tentatively.

"I think I can get you a better dinner than dandelions. Want to go to Perkins?"

"After the bunnies go home, maybe," she said.

"Okay then. When the bunnies go home, we can get chicken nuggets."

"Spaghetti," she said, correcting me. I had a lot to learn about the person she was becoming.

As the sun began to dip below the grove of trees, the bunnies went home. "Can we come back tomorrow?" she asked eagerly. She might as well have asked me if we could go to Disney World in the morning.

"I don't know. We'll have to ask your dad."

"Oh, yeah. I forgot."

We sat silently on the quilt together. I broke the sullen moment with and offer of Perkins, spaghetti, and chocolate pudding. Katie nodded her head enthusiastically. She took White Bunny and tickled my nose with it. *If only I were a real bunny mommy. She took her children home with her.* I had to hold back the tears.

Katie was a petite five-year-old, with onyx eyes and long dark silky hair gathered into two long braids. On the ride to the restaurant, I asked her, "Does Daddy braid your hair?"

She answered quietly, "It depends what house I'm staying in."

I didn't understand her answer so I asked her if she stayed at different houses with her dad. "No," she whispered, "I go alone."

61

Katie's biggest secret. Bounced around from family to family, never sure who would braid her hair. I wanted to grab her, hug her, tell her she never had to get her hair braided at a strange house again. I'd be her forever home. Her forever mom.

How in hell can I promise that when all my food comes out of a pizza box, I haven't done laundry in three weeks, and I spend my nights searching for the interdimensional portal hiding in my house?

I began to wonder if I had made a mistake reentering her life. Maybe she was better off believing in a memory not a person. *STOP IT!* I shouted at myself. *You are avoiding your own guilt. Suck it up. Deal with it. Katie has to and she's the innocent in all this!*

Mercifully, the Perkins parking lot was just at my right. Spaghetti was a wonderful distraction.

Perkins was accommodating. Booster seat, coloring book, crayons, and red Kool-Aid started us off. The truth was, I was so broke I could only afford to feed Katie. I ordered tea. Katie got her spaghetti. Then the conversation got silly. We laughed about bunnies. She told me in very great detail the entire plot of *The Little Mermaid*, including singing its sound track. By this point I was reduced to nods, smiles, and giggles. Not a bad place to be if one wants to bond with the child you abandoned.

It's a sick truth of mine. I abandoned her. I didn't do it because I was cruel or selfish. I did it because I was so ill, I would have become a bad mother. My reasons were pure. But to little Katie, I simply left her with no note and no forwarding address.

As I was listening to Katie sing "Under the Sea" and torturing myself with the list of my crimes, I heard Joe's voice. "Hi, Katie."

"You forgot to say hi to Mommy, Daddy," she said.

Her words were a salve for the wound I had just inflicted on myself.

"Hi, Tova," Joe said perfunctorily.

"Want to join us?" I asked, hoping he'd say "no." He did not disappoint. "No, I have a date tonight."

Katie innocently asked, "Where am I sleeping tonight?"

Joe looked at me guiltily, his secret out in the open. He ignored my eyes and answered Katie. "Auntie Ann's tonight."

Katie clapped. "I get to play with the twins!"

The only victim at this table was also the only person who didn't see herself as a victim. "Let's go, Katie," Joe commanded.

Katie gave me White Bunny to kiss, took Joe's hand, and she was gone. I finished her spaghetti and paid the bill. The best part of me just walked out the door with someone who wouldn't be there to braid her hair in the morning. How exactly was I going to repair all this damage I had done?

Home was now colorless. What the afternoon with Katie showed me was just how alive my world could be if only she were in it. I needed Katie as much as I knew she needed me. I drifted back to her infancy when I feared I would never be able to bond with her enough to parent her. Now I knew the answer. I had the bond but my illnesses kept me from being the parent. I had a mountain to climb before Katie would never have to wonder who was going to braid her hair in the morning.

It was time for me to take a searing look at how I had been managing my recovery since Franklin Hospital. I'd been engaging with my treatment as if I had no deadline, no sense of urgency. I was deluding myself. There was urgency. Katie's life was ever evolving without me in it. Was my window of opportunity for meaningful parenting closing? It would be dishonest for me to say that I pulled myself together in that moment for the sake of my daughter. The love was there, no doubt. But my psyche and my hope were in tatters. It would take far more than a self-pep talk to mold me into the mom Katie deserved and I wanted to be.

My daughter's and my relationship limped along. I saw her when Joe would let me, when I wasn't hospitalized, and when I wasn't wildly symptomatic. She and I never seemed to be able to graduate to the next bonding milestone: trust. Joe didn't trust me and Katie didn't trust me, not entirely. I comforted myself with the thought that she at least knew who I was. She knew I could be fun, when she got to see me. What she didn't know was that she could rely on me to keep her safe, meet her needs, and be consistent with her care.

The ugly truth was I couldn't rely on me to keep me safe, meet my needs, or be consistent with my care. Not only was I running out of time with Katie, I was running out of time with myself. I was bludgeoned with that brutal reality during a treatment planning meeting I had to attend in the spring of 1995.

The senior psychiatry resident sat across a conference table from me, flanked on his right by the senior clinical social worker. The resident, Dr. M, began, "Do you know why you are here, Tova?"

I whispered, "Not really."

"We've made a decision about the future of your care. You have shown a complete inability to adapt to life outside a hospital setting. Your symptoms have continued despite aggressive treatment. You've had five emergency inpatient admissions. You don't bathe or even put on clean clothes regularly. It's clear you need a more structured therapeutic setting than you currently have. We are considering either a placement in Morewood State Hospital for long-term treatment or permanent placement in a group home. Do you have anything you want to say?"

My hands trembled, my voice cracking as I got the words out. "I'm someone's mom. I want to parent …"

He interrupted me and said, "That is not a reasonable expectation." He stood from the table to walk out, the social worker following behind. I was left in the conference room, alone. I was now the walking dead. A treatment failure being sent to psychiatric Siberia.

Katie and I were supposed to go for ice cream that evening. I had been looking forward to it all day. She was in the middle of detailing the great kindergarten drama of the week. Something about a spilled juice box and a pink pair of shorts. I think I followed the nuances. There were only six children in her class, but you would think this rose to the level of eighteenth century royal court intrigue.

I loved it. Katie said anything and everything that came to mind. Nothing in any particular order and none of it prioritized. I had to pay close attention because she'd slip really important stuff in between telling me who wanted to hold whose hand at lunch.

I picked her up, on time, and we went for soft serve ice cream. She slipped in one of those really important comments in between licking dripped ice cream off the bottom of her cone: "Mommy, why can't I live with you?"

I put my arm around her and said, "You know how every day you go into school and learn something new so you can get better at reading or math?" I had her full attention. "I go to school too, but I'm learning to be a good mommy for you. When I'm done learning, you'll come live with me."

Staring at her cone, she replied, "Oh okay. Can I have another napkin?"

"Coming right up. Wait right here."

"Don't forget to come back," she said, and I had to fight my urge to cry.

I had lied to my daughter. I wasn't learning how to do anything. That was resident's point. I was hopeless. However, my social worker had a different opinion of the situation.

"Tova." Abby pulled me out of my stupor. "Can we talk?"

I shrugged and said, "Sure." I followed her into her office.

"I really believe that you can do better than the resident thinks you can. You need treatment for severe trauma and you aren't getting it here. This isn't the right therapy for you. Talk to your old doctor and get a referral for a respected trauma therapist. I'll help you set up the appointment."

"I can't be helped," I said. "I lied to my five-year-old. I couldn't tell her that I was being sent away from her because I was worthless. I told her she'd live with me one day."

Abby nodded and gently replied, "She will live with you one day. Let's get the referral. I'll talk to the resident."

I got the referral by calling the psychiatrist Sue sent me to. He had someone on his list he highly respected. Her name was Carrie. I sat on the referral for weeks, unable to muster the belief that this woman could make any difference in my fate. Abby made me cough up her name, and under my social worker's watchful gaze, I made an appointment with Carrie.

I had just taken my first step toward fulfilling my promise to Katie. I was no longer a liar. I was going to try to learn to be that good mommy for her.

CHAPTER 6

UNPACKING THE PAIN

I showed up for my first appointment with Carrie in more pieces than Katie's Lego sets.

I had bipolar 1 disorder with psychosis, PTSD with psychosis, OCD, and a dissociative disorder. Carrie was undaunted by my alphabet soup of diagnoses. While she was willing to commit to me, I was less sanguine about her.

The wall of distrust had a name: Sue. Carrie admitted as much. "First on the therapeutic menu," she proposed, "untangling your relationship with Sue."

I buried my head in my hands and whispered, "I wasn't good enough anymore to be part of her family. She threw me away."

Carrie carefully probed, "Did Sue tell you that you were part of her family?"

I nodded my head, my face still buried in my hands. "We did everything together. Holidays, vacations, casual family meals, activities with our children, birthdays. I even gave her Mother's Day cards and gifts that she was excited to get. She was my mom. She said she'd always love me unconditionally. Then one day she stopped loving me."

I looked up at Carrie to see her stunned face. "I know you can't hear me right now, but what Sue did was cruel and broke every psychotherapy rule. We'll unpack this. It will take time, but we'll get there." For some inexplicable reason, I found myself believing in her.

I relayed to Carrie the first time Sue told me she was my family. It was the summer of 1992. Sue asked me one session if Katie and I would like to come to SeaWorld with her and her family. I jumped at the chance. I hadn't made any vacation plans yet and the thought of spending my vacation time with Sue and her family sounded glorious. We all piled into to her new Chrysler minivan and headed for Ohio.

Katie was two and Sue's children had adopted her as their baby sister. Every time she'd fuss, one of Sue's children made it a point of getting her to giggle. They made faces at her, tickled her, blew raspberries on her cheek, gave her kisses with White Bunny, and tried to teach her songs. The entire ride, Sue's children were the entertainment committee for my delighted toddler. Katie and I had our own room at the hotel, but Katie would toddle into Sue and her husband's room where she was scooped up and tossed in the air by Sue's husband. The kisses were plentiful. The laughter made the hotel room peal.

SeaWorld itself was not too exciting. Katie was too young for Shamu or the sea lion show, but she did make friends with a gaggle of ducks, a sting ray, and a herd of penguins. For water recreation, there were the sprinklers and the drinking fountains. Katie and Sue's daughter played a splashing game with the water fountain. They both ended up soaked, cooled off, and all smiles. I was still under the cloud of depression, but Katie was having a vacation to remember (if a two-year-old is capable of remembering anything) and that brought me great comfort.

Sue turned to me, put her arm around me, and whispered in my ear, "You have a family now, Tova." I laid my head on her shoulder and wept. *Yes, I finally have a family*. I knew, in that moment, that I was loved.

"Carrie, Sue lied to me," I said.

"When did you come to understand Sue couldn't be your mommy?" she asked.

I swallowed hard. "When I realized I was lying to people about my relationship with her. Friends and coworkers would discuss holiday and vacation plans and I would lie to them, because on some level I understood that there was something not right about what Sue and I were doing. I didn't want to be judged. I didn't want to lose Sue's love. So, I just lied. It was easier."

I explained to Carrie that I couldn't confront the conflict so I split the two relationships apart in my mind. There was the basement-office Sue and there was the dining-room-table Sue. In my mind, I made her two completely separate people.

That trick worked for a while, but as my illnesses progressed and I became more severely symptomatic, the wall between family and treatment collapsed. Everything bled out from there. I explained to Carrie I couldn't play two roles. I was just too ill. I begged Sue to let me see a different therapist and she and I could stay family. Sue refused and the dual relationship destroyed both relationships. I no longer had a therapist and I no longer had a family.

I stared unflinchingly at Carrie and confessed, "I ruined the relationship. I broke it."

"No, Sue was the one in charge. She initiated the relationship. She knew you were ill and vulnerable and for whatever reason she chose the dual relationship. It's not on you." I listened to Carrie but I couldn't own it. I'd have done anything to redo the past so Sue and I could be mommy and child again. Carrie understood that reconciling my relationship with Sue would take a long time. The wound was deep.

My treatment bounced between the partial hospital program and Carrie's office. The first significant shift I noticed after treatment with Carrie began was that I had far fewer emergency admissions to the psych hospital. Abby, my social worker at the partial hospital program, was right. I needed a solid trauma therapist. Carrie was a master at soothing the abused child that lived inside of me. The more that little girl felt comforted, the better I coped with life. More than anything, I needed to feel competent again. If I couldn't learn to live as an adult, I could never be Katie's mom and I wanted that more than I wanted to breathe.

Carrie said to me one session, "If I'm going to help you reclaim your adult-self, I need to know what skills you learned as a child."

The irony of having to reconnect with my adult was that I was actually born an adult. I skipped infancy, toddlerhood, and childhood. I was marinated in the severe mental illnesses of the grown-ups in my life. Dodging the violence, sexual abuse, and neglect of my world required that I become my own parent. No one around me was up to the job.

The problem with being your own parent is you miss critical life lessons and skills. I used my extraordinary ability to dissociate and my intellect to survive. I created imaginary worlds everywhere. I had mind sanctuaries on the playground, at school, in a closet at home, and while being abused. These places of refuge protected me from succumbing to the psychoses of those around me or killing myself.

I confessed to Carrie that I never learned basic self-care skills growing up. I didn't know people brushed their teeth every day. I had no idea that other children didn't dress themselves with clothes pulled out of a maggot-infested mound of dirty laundry. I didn't bathe. After all, didn't water dissolve my skin and make me go down the drain? I didn't know food was not supposed to be eaten like my fork was a steam shovel. I just assumed everyone snuck food in the middle of the night, fearful that in the morning it might be gone. These life lessons were lost on me. I knew how to survive crazy, not how to live normal.

I explained that I kept myself sane because I always had an escape route. A closet was my secret weapon in childhood. It was located in a strange sort of room. It was off a bedroom that was off a hallway. You couldn't enter the spare room unless you first passed through the bedroom that I shared with Janet. Janet never went into that spare room. She thought it was Satan's bedroom. I wasn't worried about Satan. I was worried about the real live flesh-and-blood humans who tormented me. The spare room was a place no one ever really went into except me. The room was wallpapered in a print of baseballs, footballs, bats, and gloves. The plaster under the papered walls was crumbling and cracked. I would have preferred pink wallpaper with ballerinas on it, but when basic necessities like clean clothes were scarce, the wallpaper was trivial. The spare room was often used for storage. Boxes were piled up floor to ceiling. Assorted piles of random junk were strewn all over the floor, and an old four-poster double bed with a broken spring mattress was shoved against the wall, itself piled high with old clothing. However, in the far corner of this junk heap was a doorless closet. I emptied it out. It was the perfect place to hide in safety. I could barricade myself in with the boxes and I was protected.

In this magic space, I huddled with my stuffed bunny, Hoppity. Sometimes I would rock rhythmically for hours. I dove into my inner world where all those television programs I gorged on were recorded. I'd make up my own story plots where I was a member of the television family, sheltered, warm, and clean. Sometimes I imagined myself a child patient of one of the television doctors of the time. In my plots, the doctor always adopted me.

Sometimes I'd sit in my space drawing pictures of the Starship Enterprise. My closet became my own personal bridge. Dr. McCoy was always my hero. I wanted to be beamed up to the Enterprise, have any food I wanted magically materialize, and become Dr. McCoy's child genius assistant. I never missed a *Star Trek* episode. Just as I never missed half a dozen family shows and medical shows that were broadcast in the 60s. I would come home from school and run to this sanctuary before terror stalked me. I'd do my homework on the floor and let the sounds of screams and smashed objects wash right over me. The spare room had no light fixture, so when night came, I'd sit in the dark, rocking, hungry, and crying because outside this magic closet was where the horror lived. I mused that if my world had no people in it, I'd be safe. There were no people in my closet, and so I spent much of my childhood within its protective walls, emerging only when forced to or to watch television.

I told Carrie, "I miss my closet."

She replied, "Your closet has become your prison. If you stay in it, you'll never parent Katie." She was presenting me with an awful choice. Emerge from my safe place and face the monsters or never parent my daughter.

"I'm so scared, Carrie. I don't want to lose Katie but I can't face the monsters."

"You aren't ready to face the monsters, but you are ready to reclaim your adulthood. There is a middle ground."

That idea had never occurred to me. I could do some healing without coming face to face with the brutes that menaced my childhood. I looked up at Carrie with confidence. "I can do middle ground," I said, and I really believed it.

Carrie smiled and said, "Yes you can, and you will be Katie's mom again."

I spontaneously hugged her. I had hope for what felt like the first time in a lifetime.

Carrie was curious about how I learned basic self-care skills if not through childhood. I gave her a one-word answer: "College". She looked intrigued.

I explained to her that I had no skills when I escaped my childhood home for college. However, I was a gifted student and a keen observer of people. I learned by watching. It all started in the college cafeteria. I had no idea how to make good food choices. I came from a place where food was either plentiful or scarce. When it was plentiful, I gorged. When it was scarce, I starved. Walking into that cafeteria and facing a cornucopia of food choices was terrifying. I looked around and other students had a salad or a hamburger with fries but I didn't know where to get those choices. Instead, my eye caught the soft-serve ice cream machine. I filled a dinner-sized plate and buried the ice cream in chocolate sauce. I then shoveled it in my mouth faster than the ice cream could melt. I sat alone but I was keenly aware of the stares and chortles directed at me. I overheard someone snigger, "She'll be 200lbs before the semester is over." The table burst into laughter. I burst into tears.

I became so terrified of the cafeteria and all its food that I developed an alternate meal plan. I took a large box, went to every dorm vending machine, filled the box with chips, cookies, pastries, crackers. You name it, I bought it. Then I hid the food under my bed and I ate out of the box. I sneaked my food. If no one saw, I couldn't be shamed for it. The box also served as a source of comfort. As long as I had food under my bed, I'd never have to worry about another famine. I was paranoid that the food supply to the school would be shut down and the cafeteria would be emptied. Having my box meant I'd have food and the kids that ate out of the cafeteria would be the ones hungry. I smiled at the prospect of the students who laughed at me coming to me for food.

My box got noticed, however. Soon I began finding half-eaten candy bars and crushed chips in my bed. I'd clean off the crumbs and say nothing. This just brought more ridicule because it didn't occur to me to wash the sheets. The more I ignored the food in my bed, the more of it there was.

Then one evening, one of the girls in the dorm came up to me while I was studying. She said she knew I was smart and she told me she had gotten a D on a paper. She wanted to know how she could get a better grade. I read her paper and wrote down suggestions for improvement. She rewrote the paper and got a B+. She came up to me in the library weeks later, showed me the grade on her rewrite, and thanked me repeatedly. I told her it was no problem and I was glad it worked out. Back in the dorm, I started to notice that there was no trash under my sheets anymore. In addition, I became the de facto dorm tutor.

As I built relationships, I felt safe enough to start asking questions about basic dorm life. I asked about laundry. I noticed people brushed their teeth twice a day. I realized I was supposed to shower more than once a week. One of the girls in my dorm even helped me pick out nice shampoo. Then came the big test, returning to the cafeteria. I didn't just run to the first thing I saw. Just like a duckling, I followed the other girls around. I too got a hamburger and fries ... with a drink.

I'm like everyone else!

Late one evening, I overheard someone ask one of my dormmates about me. She said, "Tova's odd, but she's really nice and very smart." That was the best compliment anyone could have ever paid me.

"From that moment on," I told Carrie, "I absorbed as much information about being with normal people as I possibly could. All I wanted was to know what everyone else seemed to know about getting along in life." My dormmates were actually pretty protective of me. They just had to get to know me and I had to let them get to know me. The bridge was the fact that I was a gifted student. I said to Carrie, "You know, at every junction in my life, being smart saved me."

"It's not just that you are smart. You were also kind. People respond to kindness," Carrie said.

With a wry smile, I replied, "Even if I am odd."

*

Before I fought for custody of Katie, I had to have my life in order. I had to know how to plan meals, grocery shop, keep to a budget, keep a clean house, do laundry regularly, and all the other adult tasks that never quite became natural to me. I never actually managed to really develop life skills. When I had money, I'd farm out such tasks as house cleaning and meals to house keepers and restaurants. Joe and I even hired a diaper service to clean Katie's diapers. The dirty ones would magically disappear and the clean ones magically replaced them. Money smoothed over a lot of life skills gaps. It wasn't that I was lazy. The truth was I had no idea what I was doing. I preferred to leave the tasks to the professionals. That way, I didn't sob hysterically when the laundry piled up.

During my three years of single parenthood, before my life collapsed, I relied heavily on the professional services of others to make my life livable. In 1995, I no longer had the luxury of a good salary to fill in my deficits. I had to start from scratch and learn everything. As I learned each task, I had to confront the traumas that kept me from mastering them. Carrie and I took inventory of what skills I needed to learn and we strategized how I could acquire them. Being assigned a case manager would have been a natural first step and Carrie offered to help me obtain one, but I was too afraid to let someone into my house. I point-blank refused. She explained it was easier to start with clean than create clean. I had turned into a bit of a hoarder. Items entered the house, but nothing was ever thrown away. The mess so overwhelmed me, I just stopped seeing it. My solution was to not invite anyone in, especially Katie.

Carrie was in a bind. I wouldn't let anyone in to clean and I was emotionally incapable of doing it myself. Slowly, she nudged me toward hiring a cleaning company. People, she explained, I didn't know and I would never see again. It cut down on the shame of being judged. I scraped the money together, hired a cleaning crew, let them into my house, and went to the hospital program.

When I returned, the check was gone. The house was scrubbed of dirt and stains, and the piles of pizza boxes and empty ice cream containers were gone. I called Carrie in tears. "Now what do I do?" I begged her.

She said, "Now we get to work," and so we did.

We worked out a cleaning schedule. Every Sunday was scrub day. When I was too paralyzed to do the task, she helped me find ways to distract and clean. She pointed out, "Cleaning doesn't require much thought. It requires action. Many people find housework relaxing for that reason." We merged talk radio (which I enjoyed) with cleaning tasks. I could listen to the calls and hosts banter back and forth while my body went on cruise control. It worked. I could now keep a relatively clean house. I was now one step closer to bringing Katie home.

As Carrie and I systematically conquered one life skill at a time, my time at the partial hospital program was getting tense. After pronouncing me too ill to live outside of an institution, my work with Carrie was rewriting how they saw me. The staff had a hard time believing I could make such a vast improvement in in such a short time. Instead of celebrating my achievements, they were suspicious of me. That suspicion culminated in a humiliating encounter with a psychiatry resident who tried to catch me in what he referred to as a "lie about my abuse history." That was too much for Carrie and she insisted I get my psychiatric care from a private psychiatrist.

What I wasn't noticing at the time was how Carrie was very carefully nudging me out of the partial hospital program and into relying on myself for care. If I was going to care for Katie, I had to care for myself. She couldn't actually say that, because I would have freaked out. I was so dependent on the program that any threat to it was a threat to my existence. She treaded lightly. Her first move was to refer me to Yaakov Guterson, MD, a psychiatrist outside the program.

Carrie knew Dr. Guterson from her work as a staff therapist at Gordon Psychiatric Hospital. It was a large, respected, teaching and research hospital. Dr. Guterson had just completed his residency there. When I balked at seeing any psychiatrist ever again, Carrie's words to me were, "Trust me Tova, he's one of the good ones."

After meeting Dr. Guterson, I had to agree. She was right, he was. My treatment then consisted of twice-weekly sessions with Carrie and twice-monthly appointments with Dr. Guterson. The remainder of my time was filled up by the partial hospital program.

I met Dr. Guterson in November of 1995. He remains my psychiatrist in 2019. My journey with him interweaves with my recovery and my parenting. He and a psychologist named Nancy would pick up where Carrie left off.

Although my journey with Carrie ended in 1996, the impact she has left on my life is incalculable. We never did trauma work; Carrie was more interested in resurrecting the adult in me than trying to fix the abused child. She dealt with memories as they came up, but she never went digging for them. One of the biggest mistakes Sue ever made was dredging up memories, thinking that I'd somehow face and resolve them. But I didn't want to relive those experiences. I couldn't function and remember. Sue watched as I crumbled but couldn't see how her therapy style had made the pain so much worse. Carrie's strategy was first teaching me how to function then learning to heal. It was a far gentler approach. We never reached healing, but functioning gave me Katie back.

*

"You're ready," Carrie said to me as we started our session in early 1996. I looked at her, puzzled, and a little alarmed. She read my face and elaborated, "You are ready to be Katie's full-time mom again."

77

I didn't see this coming.

Although, to be fair, she had been gently guiding me in this direction for over a year. It had always been the goal, but there was a big difference between working toward the goal and achieving it. "I can't do this. I'm not ready. I'm really not. I still have bipolar 1 disorder, I still have PTSD, and I still dissociate. How could I possibly be ready? I'm still mentally ill!" I said, speaking quickly, my words tumbling over themselves.

She looked at me and firmly replied, "Yes, you are a mom with some significant mental illnesses and you cannot parent alone. You will need treatment through your parenting years. Katie will need treatment. She's only six but she's been through a great deal. However, she needs a loving home and you can provide that."

I thought about all I had accomplished in a little over a year. I'd managed self-care. I was no longer destined for the state hospital. I was living life as an adult and not a perpetually abused child. Katie and I had become mommy and daughter over this year. Katie wanted to live with me. I wanted to be her mom.

I realized Carrie was right. I would always be able to create roadblocks for myself. There would always be a reason to hold off. However, the fact was Katie needed a parent who loved her and wanted her unconditionally. I was that parent.

As flawed as I knew I was, I loved my daughter and I wanted her to grow up feeling that love. Everything else would play out as life always does, full of the unexpected.

"Does Dr. Guterson agree?" I asked.

"Yes," Carrie said.

I took a deep breath and put my best game face on. "Okay," I said, "it's time to be a bunny mom."

"Bring your baby bunny home. She needs you."

*

I wish I could say that the transfer of custody involved Joe and me sitting across from each other, discussing Katie's needs, examining my readiness to resume my parenting role, discussing child support and visitation schedules all under Carrie's watchful eye.

It didn't happen that way.

Carrie asked for permission to call Joe and bring up the idea of transferring custody to me. I assumed a lengthy negotiation would take place. However, when next I saw Carrie, she informed me that Joe was willing to give me custody and I could pick her up when I was ready. I was stunned.

"He didn't fuss?"

"He sounded relieved," she said, and I couldn't read her tone or her face. "Katie needs you, Tova."

"I'll be the best mom I can be."

"You'll be great."

We hugged each other, knowing that our time had come to an end.

This was a moment to savor, our huge therapeutic victory.

Katie was coming home.

CHAPTER 7

TRANSITIONS

I pulled up alongside the house that Joe and I had purchased during our marriage.

Joe had wanted a house so badly and I had no inner reserves to say, "Not yet." So, we purchased an old Victorian home which had some amazing features but needed renovations to achieve its full potential. The renovations never happened. I didn't care about the house and Joe was impaired. The house stayed as we bought it, incomplete.

As I stared at the three-story yellow-brick building, I realized that just like the house, I was incomplete. A sledgehammer had been taken to my psyche and the basic structure of my life. Therapy with Carrie had partially repaired the damage, but there was a lot of work to be done. I wasn't working anymore. I was living on Social Security disability checks. I was forced to move from the comfortable, upscale apartment I could afford when I was at the lab, to a run-down two-bedroom house in a neglected neighborhood. The neighborhood's one and only saving feature: it was part of the most well-funded school districts in my state. The community was absorbed by the far wealthier ones around it. Katie would attend good schools. That was worth the loss of status, or so I thought.

I realized I was dawdling. I could see Katie's face peeking through the curtains in the living room. I was making her wait because I was taking my personal register. I gave myself a pep talk as I ascended the wooden steps to the front porch. *This is right. Little girls should be raised by their mothers, not a village.* As I stood there, I noticed that the wood was rotting under my feet. *Joe, you wanted this damn house.* I tried to ring the doorbell, but it was broken. I pounded on the door with the brass door knocker.

Katie opened the door. I knelt down to hug her. She stood aloof. I sucked in my breath and asked her gently, "Where's your daddy?"

I heard him yell from the kitchen, "I'm coming. Step inside."

I crossed the threshold into another life, another time. Katie was all packed. Two suitcases with very different purposes waited in the marble-floored foyer. One contained what Joe and I thought she would need. The other was packed with what Katie thought she would need. She held tight to White Bunny and the beat-up light-blue suitcase that had all her other precious belongings. Her clothes, shoes, hair bows, and assorted other essentials, lay orphaned in the suitcase against the wall. I had sympathy for the unloved baggage.

"She's ready," Joe declared.

I turned to Katie and asked, "Are you ready, sweetie?" She shrugged noncommittally. I was acutely aware of just how traumatizing a moment this had to be for her. It was traumatizing for me and I wasn't six. "Ready to go Katie?" I chirped. She shrugged again. I leaned over to kiss the top of her head. Her hair smelled of baby shampoo and stale cigarettes. It felt like a cruel metaphor for her young life.

Joe grabbed the orphaned suitcase. Katie tried to drag the precious one but it fell over. "Can I help, sweetie?" I asked. She looked like she was about to cry, but she nodded. "It's on wheels," I said to her. "It's like it has legs and the strap is its leash."

She looked interested. "Can we name it?" she asked.

"Sure," I answered.

"Her name is Rover!" Katie announced with authority.

"Hi, Rover," I said, leaning into what she needed to make this situation seem a little better.

The two of us wheeled out and I lifted Rover into my trunk. Katie turned to Joe, gave him a hug, and said, "Bye, Daddy."

I buckled her into the front seat of my 1990 Chevy Corsica. It was another hold-over from those distant days of having means. As I pulled out of the driveway, Katie said urgently, "Beep at Daddy, Mommy!" I beeped, Katie waved, and we began our new life together.

*

The thinsulate brick-sided house we now lived in was very simple. Cement stairs, a wooden door, and a first floor consisting of a small living room and dining room with rust carpet, white walls, and galley kitchen, barely adequate. Upstairs were two small bedrooms and a tiny but functional bathroom.

I carried the loved and unloved baggage into the living room. Katie had already darted up the stairs and dove on her bed. Fortunately, I'd kept the bedroom furniture she went through toddlerhood and preschool with. Her bed was familiar to her. Her room was still decorated in Winnie the Pooh. I knew she'd want big-girl decorations eventually but I thought it wise to keep her room the same, so that it almost felt like she was coming back home, not leaving it.

It was 6pm, which meant dinner. "Katie, do you want to eat at Perkins tonight to celebrate?"

She scrunched up her face at me and said, "Can you cook dinner, Mommy?"

I felt on the spot. However, I was prepared. I had bravely conquered the grocery store earlier in the day and stocked up on spaghetti, macaroni and cheese, and tuna fish. She picked spaghetti. We had a feast. Spaghetti with meat sauce, canned spinach, and apple sauce for dessert. That would become a staple meal in our house, but no one complained.

Dinner was followed by snuggling on the couch and watching a Disney video. I'm not sure how many times Katie had seen *The Lion King*, but she knew every song and the dialogue by heart.

I took out my mental checklist. Dinner, check; movie time, check; bath, next on the agenda. I got Katie's bath ready for her and she urgently commanded, "Wait, Mommy!" And in she came with an armful of Barbie dolls, all needing a bath as well. Katie and I stripped them down and plopped them into the warm water. She declared all the Barbies were mermaids and needed to swim. I sat on the floor, laughing. I let her play till the water was cold and she was chilly. Then I wrapped her up in a beach towel and tickled her. She hugged me, hair wet and towel drenched. Pjs and stories were next on the checklist. *Runaway Bunny* was a big hit. When she was tucked under her sheets with White Bunny, I rubbed her back and sang songs I pulled deep from the recesses of my memory. She drifted off to the sound of my voice.

I prepared my own bed, climbed under my sheets, and said a prayer of gratitude that the first day of transition was a success.

I can do this! Carrie and Dr. Guterson were right!

*

Someone is tugging on my comforter.

Bleary-eyed, I looked at my alarm clock. It was 2am. Katie was standing by my bed in her purple footy pajamas and holding White Bunny. Almost whimpering, she whispered, "Mommy, can I sleep with you, please?"

My heart almost broke. "Of course, you can! Climb aboard, kiddo."

She didn't need to be invited twice. She dove into my bed, hogged the covers, and stole one of my pillows. She had no problem making herself right at home. I cuddled her and sang her another song. She responded sleepily, "Night, Mommy."

She slept the remainder of the night snug and loved. I didn't think too much of it. *First night in a strange house, I'd want some comfort too*, I thought, but it turned out to be something far more complex.

Katie was struggling. Not only did she desperately need to sleep with me every night, she also couldn't let me out of her sight. If I went into the kitchen, she'd follow me. If I went upstairs, like a duckling, she tagged right behind. She literally had to be within inches of me everywhere I went. She went to a friend's house to play, at my insistence, and she had a sobbing meltdown when we got to the friend's door.

I was in over my head.

I took Katie's behavior up with Carrie's replacement, Nancy. Carrie referred me to Nancy when I had a change in insurance. She said Nancy was perfect for guiding me through the challenges of parenting Katie.

Nancy listened carefully and then told me it sounded like Katie had severe separation anxiety. She went on to add, "Given what she's been through, it's a pretty normal response."

I started to cry. My guilt was eating me alive. "What should I do for her?" I begged.

Nancy said, "She needs a really good child psychologist. I can give you a referral. She'll want to meet with you first. You up for that?"

I responded, "It's not about me."

"That's a good answer," Nancy said.

I swallowed my fear and called Joe. Katie was covered under his insurance and I wanted him to know that I was putting her in therapy. Surprisingly, he was supportive of the decision.

*

I sat in the waiting room of Dr. Lauri Davis and Associates.

I was so nervous, I felt nauseous.

There were children of all ages sitting, standing, climbing, and running all around me. It was chaos. "Carrie's office was never like this," I mused to myself. I wasn't impressed.

Dr. Davis came out and asked for me by first name. As I stood, she came over to me and greeted me warmly. The nausea dissipated. Laurie was a slender woman, blonde hair and young. I wondered if she might be too young. I stopped myself. I was judging her when I was about to be the one grilled. I clenched my fists and relaxed them. My hands were shaking.

After we got past the introductions, she asked me about Katie. I filled her in on her behavior. Dr. Davis asked me about her infancy, toddlerhood, and early childhood. It all came out, along with my guilt and shame. Laurie paused for a moment and gently said, "You are extremely brave to come here and be so open. That's what I need from my client's parents." She confirmed Nancy's diagnosis.

"I need to do whatever I can to help fix this for Katie. I broke her. I abandoned her."

Laurie put her hand up and said, "Stop. You didn't abandon her. You had a severe illness you had to get treated. Illness is not abandonment. Teaching Katie, that is my job." I instantly believed in her after that.

Laurie got clinical with me. "Tova, children who have been through what Katie has been through go one of two ways. They either completely reject the absent parent and bonding becomes very difficult or they over-attach and suffer from separation anxiety. Katie's path is the easier to treat. There is a level of trust she has because she kept the bond with you. She needs stability and consistency, however. What's your treatment status?"

85

I told her about Nancy and Dr. Guterson. I told her I still had admissions but they are far fewer. She listened carefully and said, "I'd like you to sign releases so I can speak to your treatment team if needed. I know that sounds terrifying."

I was terrified of doing that. "I'm afraid if I'm not perfect, if I make a mistake, or I get sick, you'll have Katie taken from me."

"No, Tova. My goal is to get you and Katie on a good child-parent footing. I'm not going to hurt you. I'm here to help you as much as Katie."

"Laurie," I said, looking her square in the eyes, "I love Katie with everything I have to give. Please, teach me how to be a good mom."

Our 90-minute session was over. As I got up to leave, Laurie said, "It's my honor to work with you and Katie." And I believed her.

As I walked out of Laurie's office, I was entwined in a complex web of optimism and dread. I was optimistic that Laurie would be able to help Katie feel secure with me. I dreaded having every parenting decision I made scrutinized.

I'll never be good enough. The permutations and combinations of things I could do wrong are infinite. This is a recipe for failure.

A wave of dread flooded me as I contemplated what I had just agreed to do. As I sat in my car, slumped over the steering wheel weeping, I remembered something Carrie had said to me several years prior: "We are trying to break the cycle of child abuse, Tova. You need to unlearn everything you learned about parenting from your caregivers and their caregivers. This will take time, but it's a journey you are up for."

I realized that the path to breaking that cycle ran right through Laurie, Nancy, and Dr. Guterson's offices. It dawned on me that I could give Katie something that was never given to me ... a safe parent. That gift was worth the price I would have to pay to give it to her.

I stopped crying, clutched my steering wheel, and declared to the world, "This will be good!" And I meant it.

*

Katie's and my life fell into a predictable pattern.

I'd walk her to the school bus with a knot in my stomach every morning. And every day, like clockwork, Katie called me from school crying because she had a stomach ache. And every day, I had to tell my panicked child that she was safe at school. I'd pick her up at the bus stop and we'd have snack time together.

Laurie told me to not indulge her. She needed to stay in school and I needed to not pick her up early. "Keep a routine, even if she's upset. She'll feel more secure at school if you don't rescue her every time she becomes fearful. It's okay to let her call though."

So, I made an arrangement with the school nurse. Katie was allowed to call me twice a day to reassure herself I hadn't left her. More than that didn't give her a chance to realize she could comfort herself between calls. Less than that was cruel, because she was genuinely panic-stricken. No matter where I went during the day, I was acutely aware of Katie's calling times. I tried to be home every day at 10am and every afternoon at 1pm. I never missed a call unless I had therapy or an appointment with Dr. Guterson at those times. I would always write that information down for her so if she tried to call when I was at an appointment, she'd have the note telling her why I wasn't home. Every variation rattled her, but as time progressed, she got used to me sometimes not being home. The routine was stabilizing for her.

The unintended consequence of this schedule was that I couldn't be at the partial hospital all day long anymore. I had to be home for Katie's calls. My psychiatrist, Dr. Guterson, and my new therapist, Nancy, had been nudging me toward leaving the program, but it was Katie calling me that gave me the courage.

The day I walked into the senior social worker's office and told her I was signing myself out of the program was a graduation. These were the same people who wanted me in a group home and Katie in foster care. Here I was, walking out under my own power with my child living at home. I felt a mixture of smugness and triumph.

*

It was daunting suddenly being responsible for my own day.

I did spend a lot of time in therapy. Three days a week with Nancy and twice a month with Dr. Guterson, but my time was suddenly my own. Just as Katie needed a routine, Nancy said I did as well. We worked on developing a routine so every hour of my day was blocked off with productive activities. I was nowhere near ready to look for employment and I was living on disability insurance and child support, but I could schedule all sorts of healthy free learning activities in its place. I hung out at the library and read newspapers. It was 1996 and I had lost two complete years. Time had moved on but I hadn't. I needed to catch up with the world. I grocery shopped every day for dinner. Not because I needed to but because I needed exposure to grocery shopping and planning daily meals. I did laundry every other day because I was terrified it would pile up. I didn't want Katie to relive my childhood. I had made some friends in the partial program who had also graduated. I had friend time. I began to settle in to life without the program. I was free.

*

Everything was progressing smoothly. Katie saw Laurie every week. Laurie and I spoke on the phone weekly. Katie visited Joe on his days off.

Katie's schedule with Joe was unpredictable. Sometimes he'd show up and sometimes he left her waiting at the window expecting him and disappointed. Joe and I rarely spoke unless it was to arrange a time for him to pick her up or if I needed to beg for money for a Katie emergency. We were navigating our new lives, imperfect as they were.

Then, relapse happened.

I had been relapse-free for almost six months, but the storm clouds were gathering and I didn't notice. I stopped following my schedule. I started to relive childhood memories in vivid sight, sound, and odor. I stayed on the floor rocking all day when Katie was in school. I was so deep in trauma I didn't hear the phone ring at Katie's check-in times. I always set my alarm clock for 4pm in case I fell asleep so I wouldn't miss picking Katie up at the school bus. This one particular day I heard the alarm and screamed at myself, *Get it together or you'll lose her! Just stop this! Stop it!*

I dragged myself out to the bus stop. Katie bounced off the bus, took one look at me and snuggled up next to me. I was wearing the same clothes I had worn three days in a row. I hadn't showered. All I kept hearing were the voices of my monsters hounding me. I went through the motions of Katie's routine. She suddenly became much cuddlier and very obedient. Any small thing I asked her to do, she'd do it without question. I burned dinner. She didn't complain. I called Dr. Guterson. I was hysterically sobbing and ranting that my childhood demons were going to storm the house through the portal. I was terrified I couldn't keep Katie safe from them because I couldn't close the portal.

Calmly, he said I needed to be admitted that evening and I had to call Joe. The call went okay. He picked Katie up and told me to feel better, as if it was that easy.

I was too ill to drive. I took a cab to the hospital because I didn't trust anyone enough to ask for help. The cab dumped me off at Morgan Hospital emergency room. I was hallucinating, in trauma, and convinced Laurie would take Katie.

I was suicidal.

I needed to talk to Katie on the phone to tell her I'd be coming home and this was temporary. I needed to reassure her that I loved her. All I could see was that all the hard, hard work everyone had done to help Katie feel secure was ruined.

I'd destroyed everything.

Dr. Guterson was empathetic. He understood that my failure with Katie was exacerbating my symptoms. Reassurance and logic weren't going to work. When I was coherent enough, I called Katie. She cried, "Mommy, are you coming home?"

I choked on my own tears. "Yes, sweetie. I'm coming home to you. We will be in our house. Play mermaids with Barbies and watch *Aladdin*. I'm in the hospital and I'm sick, but I'm coming home. I promise."

Katie calmed down a little. "That's what Dr. Davis said. She said you are in the hospital because you are sick. She said sick people get better." I closed my eyes and silently thanked Laurie.

"How's Daddy's?" I asked.

"I want to come home," she whined. She went on to chatter about her day and how Dr. Davis thought she should get a pet. That was too much for me.

I said, "We'll have to think about that. When I get home, we'll talk about pets."

Katie was delighted. "Come home soon. I want a cat."

We hung up with each of us saying "I love you."

I called Katie every day. And every day, she asked if I was coming home. Every day, I said not yet. Every day, she asked for a pet. It was clear this was one hook I wasn't going to get off.

The trauma episode and psychosis resolved.

Dr. Guterson decided I was ready for discharge.

I called Katie and told her I was coming home the next day. I could hear her scream, "Daddy, Mommy is coming home tomorrow!!!" Her excitement was a better drug than anything Dr. Guterson had given me on my three-week hospital stay. I realized she wasn't broken. I puzzled over why she wasn't destroyed by my relapse. Maybe it was just wishful thinking that she wasn't. I'd need a session with Laurie to really know.

*

Laurie's waiting room became as familiar to me as my own living room. Unlike with my first appointment when I felt jarred and defensive over the bustle and chaos, now it was a source of comfort and reassurance. I knew that in this office Katie was getting what she needed and I was getting what I needed to help her. I no longer worried that Katie would somehow be ripped from me because I was an imperfect parent.

The key with Laurie was keeping the lines of communication open between her and me. She emerged from her office and gave me a huge smile. *This appointment is starting off well*, I thought. As we both settled into our chairs, she asked very gently, "How are you doing, Tova?"

I nodded. "I'm doing pretty well. Dr. Guterson did his usual magnificent job. I'm not symptomatic and I feel pretty good."

Looking genuinely pleased, she said, "That's good news. How has Katie responded to your return?"

I sighed. "She's back in my bed. She's calling me from school every day. What worries me the most is just how well-behaved and cooperative she's being. Children shouldn't have to feel like they have to be perfect. She reminds me of me." I said the words before I realized what I was saying. "Laurie, I was a perfect child because if I wasn't, I would not have survived. Does Katie feel that threatened?" I braced myself for the answer.

She gave my question some thought. "I don't think it's that she feels endangered. I think she feels responsible so she's trying extra hard to obey all the rules so you won't get sick again."

I let her words soak in. "How do I get her to understand she's not responsible for me getting sick?"

Laurie answered, "You need to talk to her about your illness so she understands. Right now, it's a big mystery to her and so, as all children do, they fill the mystery with their fantasies. Also, I've been working on this with her as well. As she gets older, it will make more sense to her." She pauses for a second. "I do think we need to talk about an emergency plan for when you relapse. How do you manage currently?"

I admitted I didn't have a plan. "Usually I wait till it's a crisis, call Dr. Guterson, and he makes the decision to admit me. It's almost always an emergency admission." Feeling shameful about my answer, I quickly added, "But I don't expect to have any more relapses, I promise."

Laurie had a dubious look on her face. "Tova, you have bipolar 1 disorder and an extreme trauma history. Relapses are going to happen. It's better to face that fact and plan for them."

I felt scolded but appreciated her no-nonsense answer.

"How did you organize this admission?" she asked. I told her that I called Dr. Guterson and when he said he wanted to admit me, I called Joe to pick up Katie. "How late at night was this?"

I confessed, "Eight or nine."

She pressed on. "Did you know you were struggling before that?"

"Truthfully, I don't see it. I mean I know when I'm in trauma, I just can't judge how deep."

"When is Katie's bedtime?"

"8:30pm."

"It's very hard on Katie to be getting ready for bed at your house only to find herself in bed at Joe's house."

I closed my eyes and shook my head. "Of course. You're right. I never thought that through. I'm sorry."

Laurie jumped in quickly. "I'm not judging you. I'm helping you and Katie so the next relapse is less stressful for both of you.

Try communicating with Dr. Guterson in the afternoon if you know you are in trauma. Then we can arrange for a safe person Katie knows to pick her up from school and take care of her till Joe can pick her up."

Safe people? "Who might be on the list?" I had three people in mind. "Joe hates being inconvenienced by my illness."

Laurie rolled her eyes and quipped, "Joe needs to learn to rise to the occasion when called upon." We looked at each other knowingly.

"Laurie, what about communicating with Katie while I'm in the hospital? How do I help her understand that I am sick but I'll get better and come home?"

"You say that very thing to her, often."

"I tried. For the first week I was so psychotic I couldn't be on the phone. After that, I called her every day. Was that enough?"

"I would let Dr. Guterson be the judge of when you are well enough for phone calls. After that, a phone call every day at a set, predictable time would be best. It will give Katie some consistency."

I agreed she was right but I reminded her hospital wall phones are kind of unpredictable. She saw my point and said I should do my best. I continued, "I have a hard rule about visitors. I don't allow any. I don't want people in my life remembering me as actively psychotic. I'd rather them just know I'm ill, in the hospital, and then when next they see me, I'm doing well."

Laurie said, "I respect your position. Katie is too young to visit anyway, but your instincts are correct."

I glanced at the time and realized that I had exhausted my hour. As I rose, Laurie spontaneously made the sweetest comment to me: "Tova, despite all your struggles, you always try to put Katie first. That's why I love working with you."

At least she doesn't think I'm my caregivers.

And she was right. Throughout Katie's childhood, I did have relapses and admissions. I tried to follow all the rules she and I discussed, but there were times when I failed. Especially in predicting in advance when I might be struggling enough to need an admission. My relapses would be a wound Katie carried with her throughout her childhood. A wound I had to take ownership of.

CHAPTER 8

PUZZLE PIECES

Katie and I were like puzzle pieces that didn't quite fit together.

One important characteristic we both did share was our temperaments. I am by nature and nurture a compliant person. Conflict freezes me. I'd rather contort myself into a pretzel than have conflict with anyone, including my own child.

As it turned out, Katie was also compliant by nature. She was a remarkably easy child to parent. I never had to raise my voice to her. If I asked her to complete a task or answer a question, she was fairly cooperative. When she would get a little stubborn about helping me wash dishes or doing her homework, all it took was a cold stare and she'd either burst into tears first then do her homework or just do her homework. I knew early on that discipline would have to be delicate or she'd melt down every time she thought she was in trouble. I reserved the raised voice for rare occasions where there was an urgency.

Just such an urgent event took place when Katie was in the second grade. I was friendly with the woman who lived in the apartment building next door to my house. Her son and Katie played together and I would often watch Aaron when his mother was working. This particular day, I asked Aaron's mom if she'd watch Katie for me. I had a doctor's appointment. When I returned home to pick up Katie, Aaron's mom didn't know where Katie or Aaron were.

Let's just say I completely freaked out.

I went all around the neighborhood looking for my second grader and her first-grader friend. The more I hunted and failed to find them, the more panicked I became. I went back to my house ready to call the police. Sure enough, in walked Katie carrying a broom. I screamed at her to tell me where she had been.

Lip quivering, she said, "Sweeping people's porches for money."

The horror of what could have happened to these two little children knocking on stranger's doors made me physically ill. I screamed at Katie to never, ever, do anything like this again. I told her how dangerous it was and I would punish her severely if she ever did it again.

She crumbled to a sobbing heap on the floor and choked out that Aaron's mom told them to go door to door.

It took a few minutes for me to register two important facts. My compliant child did exactly what the grown-up in charge told her to do, and she had no sense of how much danger she had placed herself in by complying. On one hand, how could I be angry with her for obeying a grown-up? But on the other, how do I tell her some grown-ups can make horrible decisions and disobeying them is okay in certain situations?

I made the decision to just leave her with "never go door to door without a grown-up present with her again." I know my lack of clarity confused her. I just didn't know how to address it. Telling your compliant child not to be compliant with the grown-ups taking care of her was pointless but letting her feel totally responsible for the incident wasn't fair either. I split the difference. I let her feel responsible and told her I would have a chat with Aaron's mother because what she told them to do was wrong. Aaron's mom never watched Katie for me again after that.

*

There were more mismatched puzzle pieces to explore. The house we lived in had a pretty good-sized backyard. I had always imagined Katie playing in the backyard with a neighbor jumping rope, tossing a Frisbee, or flying her Sky Dancers (dolls that rotated in the air when you pulled a cord). Katie never wanted to go outside to play. If Aaron came over, they played trains indoors. If I offered to play catch with her, she'd get a completely distraught look on her face and beg me to let her stay indoors. If she was outside, any flying insect caused a full-blown panic attack. I tried everything to entice Katie to play outside. It was all to no avail.

The more I pushed, the more terrified she became.

Finally, Laurie told me my efforts were producing too much anxiety for Katie and she told me to back off. Once I stopped nudging, Katie settled down and used all her free time to read. I enrolled her in many library summer reading programs. One year she read 100 books over an entire summer, a staggering number. She was content. I was mystified.

*

Katie and I were polar opposites when it came to creative expression.

She was tested in the 99th percentile for creative ability in kindergarten. Had anyone tested me, I'd have been in the 10th percentile. I'm a scientist. I analyze, problem solve, manipulate data, and draw logical inferences. My fantasies lived only in my mind and were never acted out. For Katie, everything she learned she learned through imagination and creation.

This dichotomy between the two of us showed up most visibly in her play. Katie loved Barbies. If they were in the bathtub, they were mermaids living underwater adventures. If they were on the living-room floor, they were princesses and princes playing out magical adventures with props Katie created from objects around the house. She could keep a conversation going between four different dolls and never forget what play voice to use.

I loved to watch her play. The problem was Katie didn't want me to simply watch her. She wanted me to join her.

Nothing made me more uncomfortable than pretend play. I was always analyzing what the doll should say, how I should hold the doll, does the doll move when it's talking, and so on. By the time I'd analyzed out all the variables, Katie was onto another adventure.

At first, I'd sit on the floor with her. That was fine, but then she'd hand me a doll named Princess Petunia who only spoke fairy language. I have to give myself credit here; I tried. However, Katie got frustrated that Princess Petunia was going to miss her ride to the fairy kingdom if I didn't find the unicorn for her to speak to. Talking unicorns were way above my creativity pay grade. Eventually, I just had to tell Katie that mommy just wasn't very good with pretend. She was genuinely disappointed and I felt awful. Princess Petunia and I parted company and Katie pouted. Her imagination had to play out without me.

She had a passion for fairies. She read every book she could find about the creatures. Fairies were always woven into her pretend play. She made up a language for them. Then the movie *Fairies* came to the theaters. It was the story of British girls who claimed they had photographed actual fairies.

There was never a question about it; I had to take Katie to see that movie.

She was so captivated I had to remind her to eat her popcorn. On the ride home from the theater, she made a grand announcement. "Mommy, I need to do an experiment that proves whether we have fairies in our house or not." I didn't quite see how this experimental design was going to be set up but Katie had an idea. She built, from milk cartons, cardboard, construction paper, glue, and glitter, a three-story home that she knew would attract fairies, if we had any. She was the expert. She knew what colors fairies were attracted to, how much sunlight they preferred, how they liked to sleep, and what they liked to eat. Then she told me she wanted to make a sugar water solution and measure every morning to see if the level of the liquid dropped. I helped her design a measuring device with a plastic ruler and an empty margarine container. Katie set everything up and made me promise I would not scare the fairies while they slept at night. She knew some nights I didn't go to bed. I promised to use a flashlight.

Every morning for a month, Katie would wake up at sunrise to measure the sugar water. She wasn't getting the results she wanted so she changed the arrangement in the fairy house by adding some fresh flowers and waited some more. One Saturday morning, she burst into my bedroom and announced, "Mommy, we have fairies! The flowers were what they were missing!" I didn't have the heart to tell her that the sugar water was probably drawn up by the flowers. I'd keep the finer details of botany from my enthralled seven-year-old. We celebrated the discovery of fairies with waffles.

*

I racked my brain trying to come up with indoor activities that didn't involve pretend play, that Katie and I could do together. I decided to teach her how to play chess.

As a child, I was a formidable chess player. I taught myself how to play by reading books about chess in the library. Even though I was entirely self-taught, I would routinely beat adults who were none too thrilled about being beaten by an eight-year-old. My elementary school had a chess club and it was the only place where I felt confident about myself. I was single-minded about beating my opponents. If I had any aggression in me, it came out on the chess board. I played chess into middle school and on into high school. I was very hard to beat. I vividly remember the Bobby Fisher-Boris Spassky world championship chess match.

I pulled out my chessboard and followed every move the grand masters made. I tried to predict what strategy they might use. This championship was my Olympics. When I moved into high school, there was a chess club and a chess team. The coach of the team approached me during club time and asked if I wanted to play for the team. The team traveled for meets and the thought of asking my caregivers for permission and then getting on a bus with students who mostly hated me, was a bridge too far for me to cross. I declined the invitation but continued to play in the club. I was okay playing hostile opponents as long as I didn't have to share an hour-round bus ride with them. I missed out on an amazing opportunity because I was too terrified to take on bullies.

I loved the idea of introducing my daughter to the game I enjoyed so much. Katie was certainly bright enough to learn so I dusted off my chess set and invited Katie to learn how to play. I was so excited at being able to share something I was good at with my daughter. Katie was patient as I explained the different pieces, how they were set up, how they moved, and basic strategies. She had a good grasp of my instruction, but when it came time to actually attempt a game, my daughter had a completely different idea of what to do with the pieces and board. She created an elaborate narrative where the king and queen were parents, the pawns were their children, the bishops were the aunts, and the knights were the family's pet horses. She decided that the rooks were wizards with magic powers and the pieces on the other side of the board were the twins of her side of the board. She said the twins had been captured and the wizards had to rescue them. My chess idea had just been hijacked by my daughter's imagination. All I could do was sit back and admire the evolving story. Katie did actually play games with me and she was pretty good, but her heart wasn't in it. I didn't push.

Since chess didn't really catch on, I decided to try board games. I borrowed games like Junior Scrabble, Junior Boggle,

Junior Monopoly, Yahtzee, and Junior Trivial Pursuit from Ann. Katie loved playing board games. Every night we'd play a different game. I tried to pick out ones that had an educational component to them. We were either forming new words, adding dice, counting out money, or strategizing letter cubes. Of course, I sometimes let her win, but more times than not she held her own. In addition, there was a block architecture set Joe and I purchased when we were married. It consisted of wooden blocks of different sizes and shapes and they were drilled with tunnels. The idea was to build elaborate wooden structures and roll marbles through the tunnels, catching them in a cup after they traveled the structure. Katie loved the architecture part of the building. She would build a whole city where she could release the marbles and they'd cascade throughout the elaborate edifices. Katie and I both enjoyed building those cities and rolling the marbles. I had finally found activities she and I could do together.

We were bonding.

But there was an unbridgeable gulf between Katie and me.

Talking about my illnesses was the single area where I could not find a way to connect with my daughter. As many times as I had been nudged, cajoled, encouraged, and pushed into having an open conversation about my illness with her, I just couldn't do it.

Laurie was right. Katie deserved to know why her home wasn't like other children's homes. She did need to know why her mommy would suddenly withdraw or stay up all night baking cookies. She lived in dread of those days when I would disappear to a hospital and she had to stay with whomever could take her. I really believed that if the words about my illnesses went unshared with her that somehow my illnesses would not impact her so heavily. However, Katie was a keen observer. She was cued into my moods and my behaviors better than I was. So why didn't I ever just tell her about bipolar disorder, dissociation, and trauma reactions? Because I really believed if I spoke the words, she'd think I wanted her to take care of me. I was obsessed with the need to not make my daughter feel responsible for me. If I stayed silent, I believed, she'd never feel like I was her responsibility. It was a delusion. Katie did feel responsible for me and I made her life so much more difficult by not giving her context.

There was another reason I never discussed my illnesses with my daughter.

I didn't want my childhood traumas to seep into her consciousness. What was done to me were not experiences I ever wanted to sully my daughter with. I couldn't tell my eight-year-old that mommy had been badly abused and that's why she curls up on the floor and rocks with a stuffed animal sometimes or why she cries when nothing looks sad, or why she panics sometimes and runs around the house securing windows, doors, and the basement entrance. I couldn't make myself that vulnerable to my daughter.

Again, it was a delusion. Katie saw everything and she understood little of it. Laurie did her best to help Katie, but what Katie needed was to hear the words from me and have a chance to ask me questions so her homelife made sense to her.

Because of my own emotional blocks, she and I never had that conversation until she was an adult. I was wrong to wait that long and by doing so, I caused my daughter needless harm. Laurie was gentle with me. She said that sometimes there are things we just can't do but she emphasized that my silence was a big problem for Katie.

CHAPTER 9

PROPERTY

I stared at his hulking form, evading his ice pick blue eyes. If I looked at him, just his gaze would freeze my body in dread. "Please," I begged. "I want to go home."

He laughed at me. "Your home is whereever I say it is, and you want to know why?" I didn't want to know why. I just wanted Hoppity and my closet. His words bludgeoned me; "You are my property. I bought you. You are mine to do with what I wish."

And he did exactly what he wished. From the age of five to ten, he owned me. I was molded to his urges. Even when his appetites sent me to the hospital with injuries, I was his property. There were a few perks to this arrangement. He bought me frilly little girl clothes, took me to restaurants, and bought me the most extravagant toys available. Every luxury came with a cost: late-night intrusions into my bed and my body. Everyone benefited from my sale. A house was bought. A car was purchased. A quarter of a frozen cow miraculously appeared every three months in the deep freezer. It was a done deal. I was a meal ticket.

I told Nancy, "Money confounds me." She looked puzzled. I continued, "It's essential for life yet it makes me feel small, helpless, and scared. Money equals him, my night stalker. Money makes me property."

I had a terribly conflicted relationship to personal finances. How could I own anything and not be owned?

Most of my adult life I lived in poverty. First as an undergrad student, then as a Peace Corps volunteer, then a grad student. Peace Corps was a good fit for my financial angst. I lived in rural East Africa, right along the Rift Valley. I shared a tiny stone house with two African teachers. My life revolved around teaching and meeting my basic needs, East African style. I drew water from the river for cooking, bathing, and washing. I cooked on a makeshift charcoal stove. I took cold bucket baths at dawn every morning. I washed my clothes by hand. I graded papers by kerosene-lantern light. I owned nothing and no one else I lived with in my village did either. I had a stipend. I spent very little of it. Everything I needed I could obtain for a few shillings. Never once, in my three years as a volunteer, did I struggle with the fact that I was property. The reason: I didn't own anything. Therefore, I couldn't be owned.

But I couldn't evade owning things forever. When David hired me from graduate school, it came with a healthy salary. I didn't negotiate. I took the first offer because the number terrified me. *What am I going to do with all this money?*

My roommate had the answer. "Get out of here. Find an apartment in a safe neighborhood that doesn't have rats. You aren't a starving grad student anymore. You have a professional job." I stayed anyway, for six more months. Corrine graduated and I realized it was time for me to move on also. I found a one-bedroom apartment in a quiet neighborhood on the third floor of a home that had been converted into apartments.

The problem with having your own apartment; you have to stock it. It was never a matter of money. I had enough. But with every object I bought, I was reminded yet again that I had been owned, that I could be again. By the time I stocked my kitchen, I was a quivering little girl afraid to sleep in my own bed. After all, everything I owned had a price and the price was paid through my flesh.

From then on, I went to thrift shops for everything. If someone owned it before me, I could live with the fact that I now owned it. I tricked myself into believing it wasn't really my property. I was borrowing it and I'd give it back. It was a fiction that allowed me to sleep at night not worrying about the night stalker.

When Joe and I became engaged, Joe wanted an elaborate wedding, complete with antique cars to transport the bridal party and a guest list of hundreds. I had to be the least interested bride in wedding arrangements history. My stock reply to everything he asked me was, "Anything you like is fine with me." When I had to purchase my wedding dress, I went by myself. I picked the first gown that fit properly and was modest. I was done. I knew that other people put a lot of themselves into this but I couldn't.

After the wedding, we moved into a nice rented town home, furnished with Joe's apartment furniture and my kitchen stuff. So far so good. However, then I became part of a two-income household, each person doing pretty well at their job. To avoid inner conflict, I stopped making any financial decisions. Joe handled all the bills and made all the large purchases. All I did was deposit my paychecks in our joint account and sign forms. It wasn't that I had all trust in Joe. It was more because the less I knew about what happened to our money, the less the night stalker haunted me. It was a survival strategy. That's how I became a homeowner, by sheer accident. I agreed to a purchase I neither wanted nor though was prudent. I consoled myself with the fact that Joe wanted it and if Joe was happy, maybe I wouldn't be tormented.

I made huge decisions about financial matters like a scared five-year-old would. When Joe and I separated, I found myself part-owner of a mountain of debt that I'd had no idea of before and no child support agreement. I knew the debt was mine. I'd signed the papers for all kinds of loans. Car loans, a mortgage, personal loans, and credit cards were all in our joint names. The sudden awareness of the problem was like taking an ice bath.

It became more real when the debt collectors started to call me at work. Sue sat down with me and all the bills and we worked out how to pay them. She told me which ones were Joe's responsibility and which ones were mine. I told Sue that I doubted Joe would take any responsibility.

Even so, I was still in okay financial shape because I made a good salary. Then I became ill. I lost my job and was suddenly living on disability income and savings. The savings dried up from medical bills and debts from my marriage. The disability check only covered bare essentials. I had to move from my apartment to a run-down house in a dying neighborhood. I had come full circle. Poverty to prosperity back to poverty.

Most people plunged into my financial catastrophe might panic. For me, it was oddly familiar. If I hadn't been raising a child, I might have been emotionally fine living on the edge. However, I had Katie and the damage our poverty caused her is hard to overstate. I said "No, we can't afford that" to her repeatedly. I was made painfully aware of just how much she had taken our dire financial situation to heart during a trip to WalMart.

We were in WalMart and I was grocery shopping. After careful price comparisons of different grocery stores, WalMart saved me enough money that I could use it for the laundromat. As I carefully picked generic brands for vegetables, tuna fish, peanut butter, and bread off the shelves, Katie came up to me. "Mommy?" she asked tentatively. She had something hidden behind her back.

"What's up, Katie?" I asked, giving her a reassuring look that it was okay to ask me her question.

From behind her back, she pulled out a ring pop. A ring pop is a lollipop attached to a piece of plastic shaped like a ring. You can wear it like a ring and lick it. She had picked cherry. Almost scared, she queried, "I know we don't have much money but it's only 25 cents. Would it be okay if I got this?"

She didn't whine. She didn't beg. She addressed me almost as if she felt guilty for the indulgence.

I felt her deprivation and it made me ashamed. "Yes," I sniffled. "Of course, you can have the cherry ring pop. Just don't get it stuck in your hair."

She spontaneously hugged me and we gave the ring pop a place of honor between the raisins and the apple sauce in our cart. The look of joy on my daughter's face broke my heart. She didn't ask for a bicycle or the latest Barbie doll. All she wanted was a 25-cent piece of candy and even that was hard for her to ask for. I felt the full weight of the financial calamity I had embroiled my child in. It was familiar to me, but looking at poverty through her eyes, inflicted great pain.

*

Sometime in 1997, a disaster befell me. My trusty washing machine died. All the estimates to have it serviced were way out of my budget. One repairman said I'd be better off replacing it. I thanked him as I became anxious.

Clean clothes were a sacrament for me.

After a childhood of picking dirty clothes out of a pile to wear to school, Carrie taught me to be obsessed with laundry. If I did nothing else, I had to make sure Katie had clean clothes. Now I had no washer. My only recourse was the laundromat. So, every week, I dragged the essential clothes that needed to be washed to a Wash-o-Matic cleaners. I couldn't afford to wash every strip of clothing that needed to be cleaned. I metered out which items I would wash based on what Katie would need for the week. I carefully picked out each outfit that needed to be cleaned. My laundry would consist of a pair of jeans I could wear multiple times and a few T-shirts. If I was going to spend money on laundry, it would be Katie's laundry. As a result, there were two piles of clothing. The pile that got washed and would be worn and the pile that would just have to wait its turn. The unwashed pile gnawed at me every time I looked at the basket.

Wash-o-Matic, as laundromats go, was remarkably stress-free. There was a living room arrangement where a large screen television and clean comfortable couches waited for the comfort of patrons. There was a chest of toys for children to play with while their parents did the laundry. The owner of the establishment had a display of sculptures molded from dryer lint. I couldn't help it; I enjoyed coming in every week and seeing what new creations people had formed. The laundromat had a snack bar where someone could order chips, hot dogs, or popcorn. The snack bar was out of my budget, but occasionally I'd order Katie a box of 50-cent popcorn and an orange drink. It was her reward for being dragged to this place at 10am every Sunday morning and forced to wait. She'd bring a book, coloring books and crayons, or her Barbies. I'd let her play while I loaded, unloaded, and folded.

It wasn't unpleasant. It was just expensive, as any laundromat would be. The financial hole I was in never afforded me the option of replacing my washer. Wash-o-Matic became a weekly fixture in our family. But the clothes began to pile up. I just didn't have the money to do all the laundry. Poverty was causing me to slip into childhood habits. I needed Nancy's help.

Nancy listened closely to my dilemma. She asked, "How much is Joe paying in child support?" I gave her the figure. She was incredulous. "You need access to more money than you are getting from him. He should be paying far more."

I shook my head repeatedly. "He'll take her from me if I ask for more money. He told me he could use my illness against me and get permanently custody of Katie if I dared to ask for more money. Please. I can't do that." I was begging by this point.

"Tova," she said, "you can't raise a child on $1000 a month. Especially when your pharmacy bills are so high."

Maybe I need to reduce my pharmacy bills so I can do laundry and pay the gas bill.

And so, I made the absolutely worst decision I could make. I decided to reduce the amount and types of medications I was willing to pay for. I reasoned that I would then have more money to take care of Katie. I wasn't making an adult decision.

I was making an abused little girl terrified to get injured decision. I was more afraid of Joe taking Katie than I was of the consequences of relapse.

My revolving door in and out of the hospital had slowed quite dramatically by 1998. Dr. Guterson and I found a good medication regimen that worked well for me. Aside from the occasional trauma reaction or depressive episode, I was holding my own psychiatrically. The fewer admissions I had, the stronger the bond between me and Katie got. Laurie was pleased, as were we. We were moving in a healing direction.

All that stopped when I decided to play games with my medications.

Once again, the revolving door began to spin. The routine was all too familiar. Laurie, Dr. Guterson, and Nancy were befuddled. Where were these relapses coming from? Katie became more fearful. Her separation anxiety got worse and no one knew that I was doing all this on purpose because I couldn't feed my child or give her clean clothes. I was in an awful position. It took me months to confide the problem to Dr. Guterson. With great sensitivity, he explained how I could get free medication from the pharmaceutical companies. He helped me with the paperwork and the revolving door stopped spinning.

During this relapse time, I made some very foolish decisions. One January in 1999, I received a home heating bill in the hundreds of dollars. I literally had seven dollars in my checking account. As I faced an impending shut-off notice, I frantically looked around my bedroom for something, anything, that would give me $320 in cash. In my jewelry box, in the bottom drawer, wrapped in tissue paper, were my wedding band and my diamond engagement ring. I also found the white-gold watch Joe had given me before Katie was born. I had promised this jewelry to Katie when she got older. I always thought of it as her property not mine. It was the only way I could justify their existence in my life.

Desperate times means plans change.

"Found money!" I screamed. I knew nothing about selling gold and diamonds. There was no internet to explore options. I had remembered seeing several pawn shops along the way to Nancy's office. These shops had iron bars, disheveled people hanging around, and the neighborhood had a bad reputation for crime. *I have no choice. I need to pay the gas bill.* I was thinking like an abused child again. My property was valuable. A jewelry appraiser was the more rational response. However, I was thinking out of a place of trauma not wisdom. I just wanted to pay the gas bill so Katie wouldn't freeze.

I stood in front of the pawn shop door, shaking. To my left was a man in dirty blue jeans and a green camouflage coat. He reeked of alcohol. As I stepped around him, he grabbed my ankle and asked me for $50. I started to cry. I told him I didn't have $50. I didn't even have $5. In a surprising act of kindness, he said, "G-d bless you ma'am."

I smiled at the man who had just moments ago frightened me and said, "G-d bless you too. We could both use His blessing."

I entered the fortress. A skinny man with wire-rimmed glasses addressed me. "Show me what you got," he ordered curtly. I pulled out my envelope, hands shaking. He examined the property. Without looking at me he said, "$220." I looked at him, mouth agape.

I attempted my version of bargaining. I channeled my inner Peace Corps self and pretended I was bartering for tomatoes. "The jewelry is worth over several thousand dollars. Your amount doesn't reflect that." He asked me how much I wanted. "I need to pay my gas bill and electric bill. I don't want my daughter to freeze this winter. This jewelry is my only asset."

He rolled his eyes, as if I was wasting his time. "I don't need your sob story. I just want a number."

I took a deep breath and forcefully said, "$600."

He shrugged. "$580 tops."

I knew it was worth way more but if I ticked this guy off, I might get nothing. I agreed to the $580. He pulled out a large wad of crisp $100 bills. He counted out five, then counted them three times. He then gave me the $80. Again, he counted it three times. A new customer had walked through the iron barred door. He was carrying an electric guitar. I thanked the pawn dealer and backed out of the shop as quickly as I could. The man in the camouflage coat asked me how it went.

I smiled at him. "Well enough for me to give you that $50." I handed the man the cash. He was speechless. We parted with no new words exchanged.

*

I'm supposed to be bright. I can puzzle my way through complex data calculations, help others strategize solutions to their life problems, and learn new tasks in a fraction of time it takes most people. The glaring exceptions are problems that come into my own life that have me revisiting childhood. The adults in my life used to say that for all my "book smarts", I had no common sense. Had I a bit of courage, I might have responded, "And whose fault is that?"

You had to experience "common" to have some "sense" about it.

There are two decisions I could have made that would have alleviated some of the financial hardship. The first thing I should have done is get a formal child support agreement. In 1991, when Joe and I separated, I should have insisted on a child support agreement. Also, in 1998, at the height of my financial crisis, I should have asked for public assistance. I didn't ask for a child support agreement when I was in a position of relative legal strength because I was so ill, I couldn't make the decisions necessary to get an agreement together. I didn't ask for public assistance in 1998 because the case worker asked for a child support agreement and I didn't have one.

By that time, I was terrified that any move I made toward relieving my financial burden would cost me my child. I was in a position of absolute submission. I put myself in a no-win situation because of fear, trauma, and relived childhood memories. We limped along financially.

The poverty cycle lasted from 1996 till 2001.

With Dr. Guterson's permission, I picked up my first part-time job when Katie was in 7th grade. I worked at a hotel registration desk. It brought in an extra couple of hundred a month and it was enough. Katie's elementary school years were financially vicious, however.

I developed some strategies along the way to cope with the extreme poverty. One of the more fun ones was saving change. In my bedroom, I kept a huge green plastic Coca-Cola jug. Katie and I told ourselves that if we ever filled it up to the top, there would be enough money to take us to Disney World. Of course, we knew that wasn't true, but it was fun filling up that jug with all the quarters, nickels, dimes, and pennies we could find and looking at Disney World catalogues. Every time Katie would get some coins, she'd run to my room, drop them in the jug, and we'd pull out the catalogues.

We filled that jug up twice throughout her childhood. There was never enough for Disney World, but there was always enough to go to our local zoo and have ice cream. From one jug, Katie and I rolled almost $300 one time. The look on the bank tellers face when Katie and I showed up with $300 in rolled coins was priceless. I explained that we had two years' worth of coins to deposit. She smiled and said, "That's a lot of work." But it wasn't work for us. Katie and I enjoyed sorting the coins up by denomination and then piling them up in groups of a dollar. She would make patterns and smiley faces with the piles. We'd guess at the final number. When we got to the very last penny and realized we were 34 cents short of our goal, we went on a scavenger hunt for the missing change. We were always successful. She and I would "high five" each other and scheme about how to spend the money. A zoo and a clothes shopping trip always made the top of the list. There was something satisfying about working toward filling that jug and it taught Katie a valuable lesson: working toward a goal can be as much fun as achieving that goal.

Poverty produced some moments of great poignancy in our lives. On Katie's nineth birthday, I planned to bake her a birthday cake and decorate it in the form of Pikachu. I was so excited. I hadn't decorated a character cake for her in years. I hadn't been able to find the energy or the confidence.

At one point in my life, I was a true artist with cake and frosting. But I felt inspired in 1999. Katie loved Pokémon, and Pikachu was her favorite. I needed a lot of yellow cake paste as well as a pattern to reproduce from. I had saved up for this cake. I had 20 dollars to create Katie's dream cake. I went to the craft shop and purchased the cake paste. *Ouch, 12 dollars.* I found a photo on a magazine cover to copy, it was free. I checked my decorating tips. I had everything I needed. Finally, all I needed was a cake mix, eggs, powdered sugar, butter, and vanilla.

I went to the grocery store with my remaining eight dollars. The cake mix and eggs were around four dollars, but the icing ingredients added up to a little over eight dollars. I didn't have enough money to make the frosting. I checked my bank account, $2.87 remained. That wasn't going to work. I ran home and lifted the couch cushions, emptied drawers, and searched the car for four dollars' worth of change. Even our Coca-Cola jug was empty. I came up with a total just shy of three dollars. I had raided the house just days earlier looking for milk money. The hiding places had run dry. I was so close, so close to making Katie's cake, but I fell short by four dollars. I thought about borrowing the money or asking Joe. Borrowing meant I'd have to admit to someone I didn't have four dollars to my name. Asking Joe was setting myself up for humiliation. All this because I wanted to make a special cake for my daughter's birthday.

I had to face the fact that the Pikachu cake wasn't going to happen.

I compensated. I bought a can of generic cake frosting and decorated the cake with yellow flowers in a brown basket. The generic icing just couldn't hold the shapes I needed to create a character cake. I never told Katie about the Pikachu cake. I didn't want her to be disappointed on her birthday. It was a lesson. Sometimes it does take money to give joy to someone. I failed to give that joy for the want of a few dollars.

Katie was resigned to the reality of our financial life. She rarely asked for anything and her acquiescence was painful to witness. I can only think of one time when she got angry over having to hear "no" over and over again. It was early spring and she had grown out of her shoes and her dresses. My friend, Ann, kept lowering the hems, but there was nowhere left to go. I needed to take her clothes shopping. It was a necessity. I sucked it up and called Joe. Groveling, I begged him for 100 dollars to buy clothes and shoes for Katie. Grumbling, he agreed but asked for a receipt. He dropped the cash off in my mailbox.

When Katie arrived home from school, I surprised her. "How would you like to go clothes and shoe shopping?" She looked at me suspiciously. "Don't worry," I beamed. "Your dad gave me money to take you shopping!"

She was so excited. She jumped up and down, clapping. "Where are we going to go?" she asked eagerly.

"Is WalMart okay?" I asked. "We can get more stuff there."

"That's okay," she answered sunnily.

I was excited. Katie was excited. A rare shopping trip with money.

At Wal-Mart, she picked out three dresses, matching socks, hair bows, and a pair of shoes, pink sneakers. I also picked up some groceries using my own cash. Katie was dancing in the check-out aisle. New clothes, new shoes, and hair bows: she was ecstatic.

The line was pretty long so she had lots of time to dance. When it was my turn, I explained to the clerk that I needed a separate receipt for the clothes and shoes. She put them in plastic bags and set them aside to ring up the groceries separately. I packed up the cart and Katie sang songs the entire trip home.

As I unloaded the bags, horror hit me. I had the groceries, shoes and hair bows, but I didn't have Katie's dresses. I had to tell her. "Katie, I left the bag with your dresses at the store."

She melted down right there in the living room. She sobbed and shook so hard, I thought she was going to break. I kneeled down on the floor and tried to comfort her. She pushed me away screaming, "Don't touch me! Just don't touch me!"

I had to do something to comfort my grief-stricken child. Then it dawned on me that the store probably had the dresses. I called Wal-Mart and begged them to look for her missing clothes. At first, they were dismissive. I pleaded, "You don't understand. My daughter hardly gets anything because I'm so poor. These dresses might not mean much to you, but they mean everything to an eight-year-old girl who hears no an awful lot." The man on the phone became much kinder. He took my name and phone number and he promised to search the check-out aisles. I told him I was in aisle five.

I sat anxiously by the phone praying he found those dresses. The phone finally rang and I dreaded the worst. But they told me they had the clothes.

"Katie!" I called.

"What?" she asked sullenly.

"The store has your dresses. Let's go pick them up." She leaped at me and gave me a giant bear hug. Those cheap Wal-Mart dresses meant everything to her. It wasn't the dollar amount. It was that they made her feel pretty and for once she heard "yes".

*

My financial status created a power differential in my relationship with Joe. He was still maintaining a six-figure salary and I was scraping by on disability and however much child support he felt like giving me. He knew I was dependent on him to meet Katie's needs, and he took full advantage of the disparity.

I knew that if I begged hard enough and I could prove genuine need, he would cough up the cash. But the constant groveling took a toll on me.

I beg. Joe fusses. I beg some more. He begrudgingly comes through. Rinse and repeat.

This situation permeated every aspect of Katie's and my life. It triggered a shame response in me and anxiety in Katie.

My situation with Joe had a name: financial abuse.

I learned the term too late in my treatment to have it make a difference in our lives.

CHAPTER 10

THE MENAGERIE

"Mommy, Laurie says I can have a pet. Can we get a cat?"

Katie's question had been expected. Laurie had already advised me on the wonderful benefits pet ownership would have for Katie. I was thinking, *Maybe a goldfish*. Katie was a few evolutionary steps higher than my comfort zone. Specifically, she wanted a cat.

As I tried to come up with a response that would buy me more time, Katie looked up at me, dark brown eyes pitifully begging, hands clasped as if G-d was going to advocate for her, and repeating, "Please, please, please. I'll take care of her."

I pondered how many moms over the centuries had seen those same pleading eyes and heard the same promise, only to give in under the pressure. I was a bit more realistic. I knew full well this cat would become my cat, and, if I was lucky, maybe, I could coax Katie into feeding her every now and then. I needed a game plan to get out of this and I didn't have one.

I knew a cat violated my lease, was out of my price range, and was beyond my ability to emotionally take on. I had a complex relationship with animals and the higher up the food chain they were, the more difficult the relationship became. It's not that I disliked animals. I actually had the inverse problem. I saw them as so vulnerable, dependent, and helpless that their needs terrified me. A puppy shaking because of a thunderstorm or a cat pitifully meowing because dinner was late would reduce me to a quivering, guilt-ridden mess. I was barely making it with a two-legged child. Taking on a furry four-legged bundle would have really done damage to my carefully balanced life. I had to tell Katie, "We can't get a cat." But I knew I'd have to offer her something enticing in exchange. I saw a long negotiation in my future.

"Katie, we can't have a cat, sweetie. I'm really sorry. You'll be at school all day and the cat will need a lot of attention we can't give her. How about we figure out what would be a good pet for us to get."

She began sulking. She really had convinced herself that she could have a cat if only she pleaded hard enough. I had an idea. "Katie, how about we go to the pet store and you look at all the animals available to have as pets and we choose that way. My only rule. Don't ask for a kitten or a puppy." The idea of going to the pet store excited her so we piled in the car and drove to Pet World.

Pet World had every species of critter you could want, spanning all levels of evolution. We studied tarantulas, fish, hermit crabs, turtles, lizards, snakes, birds, mice, hamsters, guinea pigs, rabbits, kittens, and puppies. We made a list. Kittens and puppies were off the list. I prayed hard that the tarantula and snake were off the list as well. When Katie exclaimed, "Ick, that's gross," at both of them, I knew I was safe. Katie explained what she wanted. The list of requirements included that she had to be able to hold them, pet them, play with them, kiss them, and sleep with them. All but the last one was doable.

She held all the furry rodents, stroked a turtle, turned her nose up at the fish, and reluctantly said no to the bird because it was hard to cuddle. She kept returning to the mouse cage to giggle at the way they played together. The deal was sealed when the pet store employee let her hold a white mouse and she went nose to wiggly nose with it. Katie wanted a mouse. As a bonus, it turned out mice were very inexpensive. I let Katie pick out two female mice and together they cost around six dollars. The cage, mouse food, bedding and a mouse ball all came to less than 25 dollars. I knew a call to Joe was in my future, but as pets go, these mice were an almost perfect pet for Katie.

I had a lot of experience handling mice. In graduate school, I did my research studying the effects of carcinogens on them. My research made a lot of lab mice very unhappy. Katie's new pets were a chance for me to make amends to the rodent population and it was actually an animal I felt competent to care for. Katie had picked out two mice. A white one she named Snowy and a black mouse named Lightning.

Katie was in love with her new pets. I was very flexible about her handling them. I knew the more she handled them, the gentler they would become. I drew a line at the mice sharing her bed, but if she wanted to play with them on the couch or let them run around on the floor in the mouse ball, I was cool with it. Katie would pick up one or the other of the mice, stroke it gently, sing to it, and hand feed it sunflower seeds. When she was done playing with Snowy and Lightning, she had to wash her hands. She was so in love with her new pets that getting her to change the bedding was not a problem. My job was to take a hose to the cage once a week so that it stayed clean.

Lightning and Snowy were fun to watch. They cuddled together, chased each other around the cage, ran on the wheel together, and made nests with tissue paper we gave them to play with. I had to admit, I enjoyed having mice as much as Katie enjoyed them. Then one evening I heard Katie scream, calling my name, hysterical. I ran down the stairs to find Katie cradling Lightning. At first, I thought the mouse was dead. One of the down sides of pet mice is their life span is only two to three years. As I checked the mouse, I realized Lightning wasn't dead but had developed an ulceration under her neck. She had to be in pain, and I knew my daughter definitely was.

The next morning, I called our local vet, told them my problem, and they told me their "exotic animal" veterinarian would be in that afternoon. I braced myself for the answer to my next question. The woman on the phone told me it was going to be $125. I felt sick. I couldn't pay a bill like that but Katie was devastated seeing Lightning in pain.

Time to call Joe.

He was surprisingly kind. He understood how good the mice had been for Katie. She had shared many a mouse story with him, and even he was captivated by Katie's enthusiasm for the rodents. When I told him about Lightning's ulceration, he said she'd need at least a topical antibiotic. I said, "Joe, we can't let Lightning suffer and we can't euthanize her. Katie will be crushed." He agreed and offered me $200 for the vet bill and medicine she'd need. He was true to his word.

The irony of taking a three-dollar mouse to an exotic animals vet at a cost of $200 was not lost on me. When Katie got home from school, we wrapped Lightning up in a wash cloth, carried her in her mouse ball, and went to see the vet. Katie was crying as we sat in the waiting room. "Mommy, what if Dr. Black can't help Lightning. Will she die?" she asked.

I didn't have any answers for her.

The veterinary clinic was very professional. They took Lightning out of the mouse ball and let Katie hold her. Dr. Black came in looking very dower. I remember thinking, *Please, G-d, make this go gently for Katie*. Dr. Black took one look at my tearful daughter and his entire demeanor changed. He told Katie that Lightning was bred to be a research mouse but ended up in the pet store. He went on to explain to her that these kinds of ulcers are common in her strain of mouse but with the right medicine, Lightning would be fine.

Katie sniffled. "She's not going to die?"

Dr. Black smiled at her and said, "No, the medicine will help her."

I left the clinic with a calm child, an unhappy mouse, topical antibiotic cream, and an oral antibiotic. We had spent almost all of Joe's $200. If Joe hadn't come through, I'd have had to euthanize Lightning. I owed Joe big time for this.

Giving oral medication to a mouse is actually pretty easy. I did it in research all the time. I hadn't lost my touch. The topical was more of a challenge. Lightning couldn't reach it but Snowy could. I had to separate the inseparable pals. Katie was really upset with me. She pleaded with me; "They'll miss each other and be lonely!" I assured her it was only for a week and she could give extra attention to Snowy, especially since she couldn't handle Lightning until she healed. Snowy went everywhere with Katie, carried in her mouse ball. If anyone can read the mind of a mouse, it seemed Snowy enjoyed the attention. Lightning recovered, and mouse life returned to normal.

As always happens in life, Snowy and Lightning lived their life spans. In mouse years, they had to have challenged Methuselah for longevity. Katie was sad. We gave them a solemn backyard burial befitting a first pet. As we snuggled on the couch, slipping hot chocolate and reminiscing about our time with her beloved mice, she asked if we could get more mice.

I told her, "Of course. When you're ready, we'll go to Pet World."

She furrowed her brow at me and said, "I'm ready now."

The moment of mourning was over.

Snowy and Lightning came into our lives in 1997. From 1997 till 2001, we had a steady rotating stream of male and female mice. Each beloved, each entertaining, each well cared for. Then in 2001, when Kate was 10, disaster struck.

We obtained a mouse from Katie's teacher that Katie named Freckles. Freckles, I was assured, was female. I checked just to be sure. She looked female to me. We then went to the pet store to get Freckles a companion, another female named Rainbow. Everything was normal in mouse world. By this time, Katie knew as much about mice as Dr. Black. Then one morning, I was in Katie's room getting laundry sorted and I heard the barely audible sound of squeaks coming from the mouse cage. I thought one of the mice had injured herself. I got the shock of my life when I peered in and saw, huddled in a corner of the cage, Rainbow with a litter of pups.

My first reaction was to be excited for Katie. All the years we'd had pet mice, we'd never had baby mice. I actually tried really hard to avoid that situation, but stuff happens.

My second reaction was to worry about what was going to happen next.

I knew a little bit about mouse husbandry. The first thing I did was get Freckles out of the cage. Male mice are not exactly nurturing fathers. I also knew I couldn't touch Rainbow or the pups when they were that young. The best count I did was 10 pups. Then it hit me. 10 pups, male and female, can have many more pups.

I knew I was in over my head.

I called my friend Teresa, a veterinary technician, who worked with research animals. She said pups can reproduce at a very young age. I had to separate them by sex as soon as they were weaned. I asked if she could do it. She said sexing pups was pretty tricky and I should let Dr. Black do it. I asked her what to do with 10 mice? She said, "Sell them to the pet store. Pet stores are always looking for mice."

I grimaced at her answer. "Snake food?" I knew that couldn't be an option.

When Katie came home from school, I told her I had a surprise for her. I brought her to the cage and she saw for the first time in her life baby mice. She was so thrilled. Then I told her what the plan was. We'd take Rainbow and her babies to Dr. Black and he'd separate the boys from the girls. We'd get another cage so they could stay separated, and then we'd discuss what happens to the pups when they've grown.

She barely heard a word I said.

She danced around her room declaring Rainbow was a mommy mouse and she was the aunt. I let her bask in her excitement. Then the day came to take the brood to see Dr. Black. It was a long wait but when they finally called us back, he congratulated Katie and looked at every pup under a magnifying glass to sex them. He was careful, thorough, and got a chuckle out of Katie's enthusiasm.

Then it happened, the Great Mouse Plague of 2001.

Several days after they were sexed, I went to clean the girl cage and to my horror, I found that half the babies were dead. A few more days later, all the babies were dead. One week later, Rainbow was dead. We buried everyone. I was sobbing. Katie was grief-stricken. We sat on the couch hugging each other. Katie turned to me and between sniffles whispered, "No more mice, Mommy. It hurts too much. All those babies and they are all gone."

I kissed the top of her head. "I'm really sad too. Maybe it's time to have a different kind of pet."

Katie leaned into me and mumbled, "Not yet."

I scrubbed every cage and then called Daniel (Katie's pediatrician) in case whatever killed the mice could infect humans. He assured me that was highly unlikely. Teresa had a theory that the mice were exposed to an infection brought in by another animal at the vet's office. That's why the colony died so quickly but Freckles was perfectly fine.

We were a house in mourning for a while.

A month after the Great Mouse Plague, Katie came up to me and said she was ready for another pet. I took this as a good sign.

"Do you know what kind of pet you'd like?"

"Yes," she declared definitively. "I want a parakeet."

I groaned silently. I hated birds. We trekked back to the pet store. As soon as the clerk saw Katie, he greeted us eagerly. "Another mouse, Katie?" he asked.

"No," she answered sadly. "I want a parakeet."

"I have many pretty parakeets with lovely voices. Want to see?"

And so the clerk and my daughter went off to discuss birds. My friend Teresa told me the parakeet and all its belongings were her gift to Katie for taking such good care of mice for all these years.

Katie chose a blue and gray male parakeet that she named Flutter. Katie picked out the Taj Mahal of parakeet cages along with toys, seed, treat bells, mirrors, and bedding.

This bird quickly became my nemesis.

Flutter adored Katie. He'd sit on her shoulder and sing to her. They'd watch the movie *Paulie* together while Flutter ate off her shoulder. Katie carried that bird around on her finger. He'd come to her when she called him. It was a match. Me, on the other hand, I'd go into the cage to change a treat bell or add vitamin drops to his water and he'd divebomb my finger and sink his beak into my knuckle. He drew real blood and I had to shake him loose. When he flew around free, he'd land on my head and pull my hair out one painful strand at a time. I was the victim of parakeet abuse and all my daughter could do was roll on the floor hysterically laughing. She was not going to give me any sympathy.

The only kind thing I could say about Flutter was that he made an amazing science fair project for my daughter. It all started when Katie and I were brain storming seventh-grade science fair ideas. She came up with the idea of making an analysis of whether Flutter chirped differently if exposed to classical music vs. rock music. We were a classical music household.

Symphonies or opera, we were the home for Mozart and Bach. Katie wanted to see if she could figure out if the pitch, frequency, and volume of Flutter's chirps changed based on the type of music he listened to. On three separate occasions, Katie made half-hour recordings of Flutter listening to Billy Joel's *Glass Houses* and Mozart's Clarinet Concerto. Katie scored every chirp based on pitch, frequency, intensity, and volume. She created a data sheet for each variable and carefully recorded each data point on the table. When Katie collected all the data and analyzed it, her study showed that Flutter was more agitated when he chirped for Billy Joel but also higher pitched and more engaged. When he listened to Mozart, his chirps were low pitched, infrequent, and lacked intensity. Katie concluded that while Billy Joel was more stimulating for Flutter, Mozart was a soothing influence on him. Katie got an A for the project and I warmed up to Flutter. It's good not to hold animosity toward your child's pet when he gets her a good grade in science.

By the time Katie reached high school age, we were pet veterans. We started with mice, graduated to parakeets, were gifted a bunny, and had an ill-fated encounter with really aggressive dwarf hamsters we were asked to foster. What Katie wanted more than anything was a cat, however.

I was working part-time by that point so finances weren't the problem they once were and Katie had a track record of being responsible with her pets. I offered her a puppy. Like every pet Katie and I have taken on, we did our research. Katie wanted a dog she could do agility course training with. I consulted Teresa and she recommended a Shetland Sheepdog. Katie was serious about doing agility and although it wasn't a sport I knew much about, Teresa was actively involved and was willing to mentor Katie.

Finding Shetland Sheepdog puppies proved more of a challenge than I expected. I called the humane society and they, not so politely, informed me that pure breed dogs rarely end up at their facilities. She told me they had many wonderful mixed breed dogs available for adoption and they would be good at agility as well. She wasn't exactly nice to me. I realized I had just become an unwitting pawn in the pure breed versus mixed breed fight. I wanted no part of this squabble. I just wanted a good agility dog for my daughter who has asked for very little in her childhood. If she wanted a Shetland Sheepdog, I was going to get her one. Being guilted into a different selection because there was a raging conflict in the dog world was not my problem. Little did I know that when I agreed to bring a dog into my home, I was also inviting in a whole dog culture.

After many phone calls and newspaper searches, I found a breeder about three hours from our home. Katie was one step ahead of me. She begged Joe to take her to pick up her new puppy. Joe liked dogs. He also wanted a say in the kind of puppy chosen. He tried to nudge Katie into a different breed of dog, but Katie had become the immovable object.

The only weekend Joe had free happened to also be the first weekend after Hurricane Ivan. The roads were treacherous. Katie begged me to accompany her and Joe to get the puppy. She explained, "I want my mom and dad there when I get my first puppy." I asked Joe and he grudgingly agreed. Katie would get her family moment, although I did feel a bit like a hostage victim. The ride to the breeder was kept cordial by Katie's excitement and my desire to keep the focus on Katie's big moment. We arrived at the breeder and it was not what I expected. The owner had a number of different breeds and two Shetland Sheepdog puppies. One puppy, a female, took one look at Katie and ran to hide. *Well, that introduction didn't go well*. The second puppy approached Katie cautiously but as Katie kneeled down to pet the little guy, he nudged her, licked her, and his tail wagged energetically. Katie chose this puppy as her pal and named him Frodo, after her favorite hobbit. Joe and I approved of Frodo. Frodo appeared to approve of us.

Out came our long list of questions. We asked everything from veterinary questions to behavior questions. The woman seemed taken aback that we were so thoroughly prepared. If I was bringing a puppy into Katie's and my life, I needed as much information on the puppy as I could possibly get.

The first question I asked was about the puppy's living situation. "I see concrete and fenced kennels, has Frodo ever been out on grass?" I asked.

The woman got defensive. "No," she said, bristling. "There isn't a lot of grass around here. He's used to concrete."

Our first challenge is getting Frodo to play on grass.

I began to have suspicions that Frodo would have a lot to adjust to. Once Katie and my questions were exhaustively answered, I signed the papers, paid for the puppy, and let Frodo explore the area leading up to the car. Which was, by the way, grassy. The woman gave me his puppy blanket. Katie sat in the back seat with Frodo, his puppy blanket spread in her lap. On the ride home, Katie spent the three-hour trip cooing and talking to her puppy. Frodo fell asleep in her lap. This was a very good start.

Teresa was my go-to dog expert. I trusted her. She was a veteran of dog ownership, and she was a veterinary professional. I finally had someone I could call at all hours and ask puppy care questions. The grass issue was more of a problem than I anticipated. He was terrified of his leash so I'd attach it and carry him to the back yard where grass was plentiful. The poor little guy shook. I let him stand in the grass for a few minutes and I scooped him up and brought him inside. Over a series of days, several times a day, I exposed him to the grass. He used my cement backdoor stoop to do his business, since he was used to concrete. It took about a week, but eventually Frodo started exploring the grass and I began trying to train him to do his business on grass rather than concrete.

I had a schedule. Every three hours, including in the middle of the night, I'd bring him outside on his leash. This was tedious, to say the least, but I was potty-training a baby. Tediousness was part of the process. He learned quickly to signal when he needed to go out. I eventually got some sleep. The job of house-training a puppy is really an act of bonding. Frodo was learning to trust me and I was learning patience. It wasn't lost on me that as I was training him, I was training myself.

As time passed, Frodo began to grow into a very loving and nurturing dog. I told Katie I'd do house-training but she had to do obedience-training. So began a series of classes, puppy obedience, obedience, and intermediate obedience. By the third course, Frodo acted like the gifted kid in the class who couldn't figure out why all his other classmates were so slow. Teresa thought he was ready for puppy agility. Katie was beside herself with excitement. However, after two puppy agility courses, it was clear that we had the one Shetland Sheepdog that wanted nothing to do with agility. Every activity on the course, he'd either snuggle in and nap or approach it as a play toy. It was clear that Katie's and my dog was an agility training flunky. We snuggled him up and took him home. At the age of one year, he was retired. We didn't mind. He was meant to be a Bassett Hound not a Shetland Sheepdog. We loved him up anyway.

Looking back on this long chain of pets, I realized I had come full circle. That first day when Katie begged me for a cat, I couldn't imagine ever being emotionally equipped to take on ownership of an animal as complex as a cat. From the time Katie was six till the time she was 14, we were slowly building up to getting her, if not a cat, then a dog. Every step along the pet evolutionary ladder gave me more confidence that I could really care competently for a furry creature. Every species we graduated from bonded me and Katie closer together. She saw that I took her animals just as seriously as I took her.

Laurie was right. Getting Katie a pet was the best prescription anyone could write. All those mice, birds, hamsters, bunnies, and finally a dog, helped heal Katie and me.

CHAPTER 11

PEANUT BUTTER AND JELLY SANDWICHES

I sat at a round wooden table in my elementary school cafeteria, alone and clutching my paper lunch sack. There was a lone peanut butter and jelly sandwich and two pennies wedged under the flap of the bag's bottom. Dilemma time. Do I stand in the milk line to get my carton of milk and leave my precious sandwich to guard my chair, or do I take my sandwich with me, get my milk, and eat standing up? It's a tough decision when you're six. Everyone stares at you when you have to eat standing up. It means no one wants to make room for you at their table. I decided I'd rather risk losing my sandwich than give other kids another reason to taunt me. The line was long. I kept a close eye on my beloved sandwich. Much to my horror, children started to take up seats at my table. Silently I begged G-d that they not throw my sandwich away. I was desperate for the line to move faster so I still had food to eat. As I got to the front of the line, I handed the hairnetted lunch lady my pennies and she gave me my milk. I dashed back to my sandwich which was mercifully still there. No one said a word to me. However, they snickered amongst themselves that "dirty Tova" was stinking up their table. I listened as they exchanged apples, cookies, snack cakes, and graham crackers with each other. I had nothing to offer except my sandwich. Bravely, I offered half my sandwich to anyone who wanted to trade something with me. The pigtailed girl across the table from me mocked, "It's probably moldy." Everyone laughed. I swallowed my tears and my sandwich, washing them down with my milk.

I told Dr. Guterson once that all I ever wanted growing up was for someone to share my peanut butter and jelly sandwich. In five years of elementary school and three years of middle school, no one ever accepted my invitation. Looking back, you could hardly blame them. I was abused, unkept, poor, without any social skills, and painfully shy. In the rough-and-tumble world of public school, I was sacrificial lamb. What I remember most about the torment is that it was unrelenting. Whether it was recess, lunch, reading, library, or gym, the barrage of punches, kicks, taunts and saliva went without abate. I escaped as best I could into my fantasy worlds. The deeper I crawled inside my own mind, the less I noticed what was being done to me. At home I'd be asked how my dress got torn or why my knee socks were bloody and I'd answer truthfully; "I don't know." I was lectured about how expensive clothes were and how I'd have to wait to get another pair of socks. I turned them inside out. That seemed like a reasonable solution. I can't even say I was lonely. The truth was I was drowning and lonely would have been a luxury.

G-d gave me a great gift when I entered high school. My cousin Chaim would be in almost all my classes. Chaim and I grew up together. No one could make me madder and no one was a better friend. He was everything I wasn't. He was athletic, good-looking, charismatic, and on the A-list of our high school's social register. What we shared was gifted academics and a fierce loyalty to each other. No one dared mess with me when Chaim was within earshot. He protected me while at the same time he teased the heck out of me. I felt so safe with him I'd throw barbs back at him. Every Tuesday night we'd play chess at his house and every Tuesday night he tortured me with punk rock music when I beat him. His high-school hijinks were legendary. The number of times I had to bail him out with a teacher was cringingly frequent. Chaim used to say, "You're such a goody-two-shoes, you can get away with anything." I wasn't amused.

One particularly egregious moment happened our sophomore year. We were enrolled in an unusual gifted class. It was a combined U.S. History and American Literature class. The double class was split by lunch. As Chaim and I walked to the cafeteria, he told me that he'd forgotten his baseball uniform and was going home to get it. I told him he was crazy and no one escapes high school alive in the middle of the day with Mr. Rice waiting for us. He shrugged and simply said, "Cover for me, cuz."

When I got back to class, Mr. Rice, right on cue, took attendance and Chaim was missing. Our history teacher turned to me and asked, "Where's Chaim, Tova?" I squirmed in my seat, stared at my hands, and looked like a deer caught in the headlights. Mr. Rice motioned me to follow him into the hall. Panic set in. Just as I began verbally tap dancing, down the hall came Chaim, carrying his baseball uniform. Mr. Rice looked at us, his two best students, waved his hands, and exasperated, said, "I really don't want to know." Chaim bought me pizza on chess night. I told him he owed me ice cream too.

Chaim was killed in a car accident our junior year in high school. His death triggered my first psychotic-manic episode. I was manic at 16 and without my best friend, my buffer, my translator. Chaim translated the world of high school for me. More than anyone in my life, past or present, he knew what I had lived through and he didn't just protect me, he educated me in how to get along with people despite it. It's been 42 years and the loss is still fresh and impactful. I miss Chaim like nothing else in this world.

As Katie progressed through elementary and middle school, I prayed hard that she, unlike me, would have someone who wanted to share her peanut butter and jelly sandwich and there would be a Chaim in her life. There is no pain worse than watching your history repeat itself in the life of your own child. And history did repeat itself.

I picked my house, not just because I could afford the rent, but also because it was part of one of the wealthiest school districts in our state. Katie was gifted by all objective test measurements from kindergarten. Her teacher told Joe she hadn't seen a child this talented in math in years. Katie went to private kindergarten. Given the turmoil in her homelife, Joe and I agreed that this particular school and curriculum would suit her best. We were right. She thrived academically and held her own socially. Then the transition to a large, wealthy, public elementary school loomed on the horizon.

The switch was a psychic shock for her. Gone were the nurturing waters she had thrived in. Now she was in a shark tank and she had no way to emotionally protect herself. She had severe anxiety, painful shyness, poverty, a mentally ill mother, and an indifferent father. Katie had become the next-generation sacrificial lamb.

The daily taunts, the isolation, and outright meanness of her classmates would often have Katie coming off the school bus, running into my arms, and burying her tear-streaked face into my chest. As many times as I went to the school and asked for a meeting with the guidance counselor and vice principal, I never got that meeting. I was being ostracized for pointing out the flaws in their paradise. Instead I started getting notes from the first-grade teacher that Katie wasn't performing at grade level and should be tested for a learning disability. I was furious. Katie had already been tested as gifted. *What in hell is this teacher talking about?!* The answer was self-evident, Laurie said. Katie was too anxious, too taunted, and too withdrawn to participate meaningfully in class. The problem wasn't Katie's intellect. The problem was an elementary school that refused to hold bullies accountable.

Katie's torment came to a head in the second grade. She was invited to the birthday party of one of the little girls chiefly responsible for the distress. She lured Katie to the party with promises she wanted to be friends and say sorry. Katie was delighted to be invited to a party, her first since kindergarten. She was sure that Emily would now be her friend and she wouldn't be picked on so much. Her hopes were dashed pretty quickly. At the party, Katie was made the butt of Emily and her friends' taunts. They repeatedly tripped her when they played a blindfold game. They shoved cake in her face so hard it ended up in her nose. They asked her embarrassing questions in a word game and when she refused to answer them, they humiliated her. Finally, when the party guests had enough of tormenting Katie, they left her alone in the house as the group went to play at a local playground. Katie told Emily's mother she wanted to go home before the girls returned. I dashed over to pick my daughter up. I couldn't believe her condition. She still had smashed cake on her face. She sat on the stoop rocking silently, her head in her hands. When I knelt next to her and gently whispered her name, she didn't acknowledge my presence.

This went way beyond bullying.

What those girls put Katie through was psychological abuse. I stroked her hair and told her I'd be right back. I wanted to talk to Emily's mother. I knocked on the door and she answered, fake smile and compliments about Katie. In the most mild-mannered voice I could muster, I sliced into her. "Normally when a seven-year-old has a party, there is an adult in charge to make sure everyone is acting appropriately. I can see that this party had no adult." When she stammered that she was supervising the party I replied, "Just as I suspected, there was no competent adult home." She looked shocked. But I wasn't done. "I have a traumatized seven-year-old to take home and soothe. Katie will be fine. No thanks to your great supervision. However, you have a much bigger problem. You have a monster on your hands." I left the woman, mouth agape. I literally picked Katie up and carried her to the car. She began to sob, an appropriate response.

When we got home, I gently cleaned the cake off of her face and out of her nose, then we snuggled on the couch. Katie curled up in my lap, buried her head in my shoulder and pleaded with me to explain why they did those things to her. Through my own tears, I softly said, "Some children are so empty inside they only feel something when they are inflicting pain on others." She looked up at me and I kissed her forehead. "Katie," I continued, "if Emily so much as gives you a funny look, I'm going to drive to your school, barge into your principal's office and demand he talk to me, even if I have to sleep there all night."

Katie giggled. The thought of her mother having a sleepover in the principal's office amused her. She threw her arms around me and I saw the hint of a smile. I took perverse pleasure in the fantasy that Emily probably wasn't smiling at that moment. When Katie next saw Emily, she was a much-chastened child. Apparently telling an upper-middle-class mother she's raising a monster has an effect. I decided I'd have to remember that line if, heaven forbid, I ever had to use it again.

*

The taunting and harassment were woven into the fabric of Katie's elementary school years. However, in third grade there was a magical occurrence. Katie struck up a friendship with a little boy named Justin and Justin had a friend named Nate. The three of them became inseparable. Katie was always at Justin's home and Nate often joined them. Justin's house was appealing because it had a trampoline, swimming pool, and pinball machines, a child's paradise. I liked Justin's mom, Beth. She worked in the sciences as well so it was an opportunity for me to share my education and training with someone who could appreciate it. Beth often made me tea as the kids chased each other around, laughter pealing out of their pink cheeks. As the friendship of the trio blossomed, Katie transformed. Even though the taunts at school didn't stop, Katie weathered them better. Then one day, one of Katie's tormentors turned on Justin and called him names for playing with a girl. Katie boldly told her tormentor to leave Justin alone and playing with girls was "way better than playing with you". Laurie gave Katie a standing ovation and I gave her a high five. Katie stood up for herself in order to stand up for a friend. It was a proud mommy moment.

Sometime in the middle of Katie's fourth-grade year, I got a phone call from Beth. She didn't call me often so I knew something was up. "Hi Beth, what's up?" I asked.

She paused for a moment and then in a subdued voice replied, "Nate has been diagnosed with bone cancer. He's in Children's Hospital on the cancer unit. Justin wants to visit him. Would Katie like to come as well?"

Without a single second's hesitation, I said, "Oh my, of course. Does he need anything?"

Beth replied, "Just his friends."

"He can count on Katie," I said.

I didn't know quite how to prepare Katie for what she would experience. I called Laurie. She reassured me that kids don't get awkward in these situations the way that adults do. She told me to "just let Katie be Katie." It was probably the best advice she could have given.

Beth drove the four of us to Children's Hospital. Justin and Katie were oblivious to where they were. We shepherded our duo through the halls, onto the elevator and up to the fifth-floor cancer unit. Nate was in bed playing a video game, IVs and monitors surrounding him. My heart went out to his mom, who was sitting in a recliner the hospital has for parents. Nate's mom greeted us with enthusiasm. Her only instruction to Katie and Justin was to not jump on the bed because Nate had just had surgery. The children understood. They then proceeded to ignore us and engage themselves in a game of Pokémon. They argued, laughed, called each other dumb names, and were clearly unaware of what was going on around them. Justin and Katie wanted to play Nate's video game and after some tussling over who would go first, Nate and Justin were chivalrous and let Katie go first. The trio played, talked and giggled till the nurse came in and told us we needed to leave because the doctor was here. Katie and Justin said their goodbyes. Beth and I hugged Nate's mom. She followed us out, and with tears in her eyes, she said, "This was the best medicine Nate could have received. Please come back." Beth and I promised her the children would be back and to just let us know when.

We guided the duo back to the elevator and out to the car. Beth and I said nothing to each other. Each of us was lost in our own thoughts about the visit. Katie and Justin talked quietly in the back seat.

I called Laurie when we got home. "You were right," I said. "She was oblivious to Nate's condition. Kids are remarkable creatures."

Laurie said, "Yes, they are. That's why I love my job."

"Thank you, Laurie, for everything."

I could hear the smile in her words. "My pleasure, Tova."

*

Nate finished his treatments and the trio resumed their routine. Middle school was looming on the horizon and that would mean life altering changes for all three children. As the end of fifth grade approached, the relationship between the three of them altered. Nate and Justin were becoming more adolescent boys and Katie was becoming more adolescent girl. When they found out they'd all be on different "teams" when they entered Willow Wood Middle School, the news was met with resignation. Katie moped. Her best friends of three years weren't going to be her best friends anymore. I promised Katie she'd have new best friends. She believed me. As it turned out, I told her a lie. The vicious bullying would return and this time Katie had no allies.

Another life-changing event occurred simultaneously. Laurie, her long-time therapist, was leaving for California. It was a devastating loss for both Katie and me. I had come, over the years, to feel safe with Laurie. I brought her my parenting challenges and successes. She guided me through the former and celebrated the latter. Laurie was my security blanket. For Katie, she was losing her comforter, her ally, her compassionate listener. It was a blow of momentous proportions. Laurie referred us to a new child psychologist, but Jenny was not Laurie. Katie was slow to accept her and often wanted me to come into her sessions with her to feel comfortable. I was caught in a bind. Katie was clearly reacting to Laurie's departure by not giving Jenny a chance, but she also wasn't getting what she needed out of treatment, the opportunity to work out her issues with me. I decided to let the relationship develop and pay close attention to how Katie was adjusting. With middle school in the near future, having a therapist was just as important as when she entered first grade.

*

As I walked into Willow Wood Middle School, the first thing that caught my eye was a large red and white banner stretching across the quadruple doored entrance of the school. The banner read "Bully-Free Zone". I didn't know if this made me feel better or suspicious. The school was huge. Four elementary schools fed into one middle school and the sheer chaos of that many adolescents crammed into one building for six hours a day gave me pause. Katie was anxious but she was willing to give the new school a chance. The awful truth was the school wasn't willing to give Katie a chance. She had been labeled as "learning disabled" by her elementary school and the label was never removed no matter how fiercely I presented facts that challenged their judgement. She was lost in a building where she rarely ran into anyone she knew and was put in classes that didn't meet her needs. Katie reverted to what she knew best: anxiety and fear.

That was like blood in the water for the middle-school sharks. The torment of Katie began.

For four months, Katie endured a kind of hell no child should be subjected to. "Bully-Free Zone" was bull-crap. Instead of dealing with the abusers, the school isolated Katie. She was told to eat her lunch in the guidance counselor's office because they couldn't prevent the little Brandons and Brittanys from throwing her lunch in the garbage, tripping her while in line for a hot meal, or pushing her on the floor to take her seat. If I packed a lunch, they'd come up behind her, grab the sack, and smash her sandwich. Katie never got a meal at that school.

Outside the cafeteria, things were no better. Her homework was stolen and ripped up before she could turn it in. Her locker was routinely emptied and the contents kicked down the hall as onlookers laughed and kicked her belongings around further. Pictures were drawn of her and labeled with the vilest language adolescent bullies could dream up. Katie was brutalized on the bus ride home. The students would surround her, push her in circles, and slam her into the bus. One time they hit her head into the bus so hard, they bent her glasses and cut her face.

No adult charged with responsibility fulfilled those responsibilities.

I offered to leave work early and pick her up from the bus stop. Katie didn't want me picking her up at the bus stop. She said my presence would make the problem worse. Instead, we decided I'd drive her both ways to school. Every drive to school, there were piteous pleas to not make her go. Every ride home was accompanied with gut-wrenching sobs. She was being brutalized and nothing I did, said, or screamed at the school officials made one iota of difference to this "Bully-Free Zone" hellhole.

The bullying metastasized from the school to our neighbor-hood. If Katie was walking on the sidewalk and a group of children were there, they called her foul names that 11-year-old children shouldn't know. They threw rocks at her. In one incident a group of the delinquents ganged up on her and pelted her with ice balls. One hit her in the face and damaged her eye. I had to take her to the emergency room for treatment. At home I started to get disgusting crank phone calls that rivaled the language of the neighborhood thuglets. The bullying had spiraled out of control.

After enduring several months of this onslaught, Katie retreated into a deep depression, spending hours hiding in her room, reading. She wasn't reading because it was pleasurable. She was reading to escape the unrelenting brutality.

In December of 2001, after Katie finished her appointment with Jenny, Jenny called me into her office. I stared at her searing with guilt, pain, and powerlessness. She looked directly at me and with alarm in her voice said, "Tova, pull her from that school, now. I rarely tell parents to pull their bullied children, but in this case, when the house is on fire, you get out of the house."

She didn't have to say it twice.

Jenny said she'd handle the paperwork. I asked, "Where should I send her?"

Jenny replied firmly, "Homeschool her, cyberschool her, private school her, just get her out of Willow Wood."

I walked into Jenny's waiting room, lightly asked Katie if she was ready to leave, and listlessly she took my hand, just as she did as a toddler. My agony was only exceeded by Katie's suffering.

I snuggled up with her on our couch and asked her to look at me. "Sweetie," I said gently, "as of right now you will never have to go back to Willow Wood again."

She looked confused. "Where will I go to school?" she asked.

I kissed her forehead and said, "We'll figure that out together."

When I called Joe to tell him about Jenny's recommendation and my decision, he was adamant. Katie had to go back to Willow Wood and fight it out.

In that moment, I found my backbone. "No, Joe. She will never return to that sewer and there is nothing you can do to me that is going to change my decision. Even if you take custody away from me, you don't live in this school district so she's still free."

Surprisingly, he backed down.

From that moment, events sped up in rapid succession. The school district, probably fearing a lawsuit, called me repeatedly offering Katie all kinds of protections and safeguards. I was promised, that "the situation will be dealt with". I was now in a position of power to advocate for my daughter.

"Your school is a cesspool. I don't allow my daughter to go to school in a cesspool. Don't call me again," was my common answer to the calls. But they kept coming. I kept saying no. No isn't a word I practiced very much so it was satisfying to practice it on the school district's administrators. I felt in control.

Finally, I was really taking a stand for my daughter. It was a transformative moment.

Watching Katie live through what I remembered living through flung me into emotional chaos. I was deeply traumatized by Katie's trauma and there were times where I couldn't separate what was done to me from what was being done to her. In Dr. Guterson's office, I had several severe trauma reactions where I reverted to being a child and reliving some of the gross abuses I had lived through in school. I was always one psychotic thought away from an admission to the hospital, but given Katie's precarious condition, that was not an option. He had to find a way to keep me from becoming psychotic and further traumatized. Not just for my sake, but also for Katie's.

He added a medication for trauma that he didn't like to use, increased my main antipsychotic, and he upped my sessions to once a week. He told me to keep him in the loop about Katie's schooling and he strongly opposed me homeschooling her. He called it a "non-negotiable".

Joe and I explored our options. Homeschooling wasn't a viable choice. First because Dr. Guterson was dead set against it, and also because Katie needed to know she could be separate from me and be safe. If I became her everything, she'd never learn that critical lesson. Joe pouted and fussed because the burden of private-school tuition fell to him. I felt no sympathy for him. I was saving MY child and he just had to suck it up.

It was tough finding a private school that would take a child in January. After a number of interviews, I settled on Northview School. It was a tiny school wedged in the back of a church. But, thankfully, it wasn't a religious school. It just rented space from the church. The class size was tiny. The sixth-grade class consisted of eight students. Katie spent a day at the school checking out mainly the other kids. She said everyone seemed friendly enough. I asked her, "Shall we try it?"

Listlessly, she muttered, "Sure."

I said a prayer that this school would be healing for her.

*

Second semester sixth grade was more about recovery than academics. Katie made a friend, Kim, and that was a huge accomplishment.

Kim was a child who had suffered her own wounds in the brutal world of public school. Katie and Kim bonded over shared history. I remember Katie telling me about a girl in her class who kept sitting next to her, talking to her all through the day, and getting her in trouble with the teacher. At first, Kim annoyed Katie with her constant chatter, but she wore Katie down and they became, what turned out to be, life-long friends.

There were no instances of bullying that semester. Although Katie was more like a refugee than a new student, she soaked up the academics and began to catch up with her class. Her classroom teacher made a point of telling me how naturally bright she was. The school atmosphere was very informal. The children called teachers and administrators by their first names and the staff stressed to me that every child had a safe place to grow and learn at Northview School. They welcomed Katie and treated her with a kind of sensitivity I had forgotten schools could be capable of. Northview School was a good match. There was no good reason, except divine guidance, that we found such a precious well of compassion in a vast wasteland of indifferent schools.

When I think back at our horrid experience at our public school, I can only come to the conclusion that it was a combination of our poverty, my illness, and Katie's special circumstances that made the school district conclude Katie, and by extension me, were not worth their time. The school district had every financial and academic resource available to help Katie. What it had done, however, was lose its soul and sacrifice a child on the altar of its own prejudices.

At Northview School, Katie found children to share her peanut butter and jelly sandwich with. Her metamorphosis from sixth to eighth grade would be nothing short of miraculous. Katie was not doomed to repeat my journey. She did, in fact, have her own trail to blaze.

CHAPTER 12

SONGBIRD

"Mom! Mom!" Katie yelled for me from the dining room. I dashed down the stairs expecting to find some kind of catastrophe. Instead, there was Katie, sitting at the dining-room table staring at our latest copy of the Penny Pincher. *Ah, she wants me to buy something for her.*

Since the flier is a collection of used items up for sale, it could have been anything from baby clothes to a car. I stifled a giggle as her enthusiasm grew. "Come see this!!!" she pleaded. I picked up the flier and in the lower right-hand corner was an advertisement that began, "Seeking singers for the well-known all-girls touring choir, AGTC, ages eight through 18." Katie, pointing at the ad, squealed, "I want to audition. I want to sing in this choir!"

Speechless, I needed a moment to collect my thoughts.

There were a few problems with Katie's eagerness. First, I didn't know if this was a legitimate organization. *Penny Pincher has a lot of great stuff, but also some less than savory sources.* Second, I had no idea if Katie could even sing. Truthfully, I never paid much attention to the quality of her voice. We'd sing washing dishes, in the car, she'd sing in the shower, but it never occurred to me to evaluate her talent. If this ad was for real, what if Katie didn't sing well enough to pass the audition. She'd had enough rejection, volunteering her for more was just downright cruel. Lastly, "professional touring choir" sounded very expensive. I puzzled over how in the world I was going to pay for this organization. Joe was not exactly willing to cough up money even for necessities. I was dubious he'd pay for such an expensive recreational activity.

This would have been a Laurie moment. However, Laurie was now in California and Jenny, Katie's new therapist, was not so generous about parent phone calls. I answered Katie's elation with a noncommittal Mom answer: "Honey, let me look into this first."

This satisfied her, at least for the moment.

I called the contact number from the ad. Of course, I got an answering machine. "You've reached AGTC, the city's premier all-girls touring choir. My name is Rachel Dunlap, the director. Please leave a message and I'll return your call as soon as I can." There were some positives in this recording. The information on the ad matched the information on the recording and the message at least sounded professional. I left my name, Katie's name and age, and my return number.

Mrs. Dunlap called me later that evening. "Ms. Feinman? I'm Rachel Dunlap from AGTC. I understand your daughter Katie would like to audition for our 2001 fall semester."

"Yes, she would. Ever since she saw your ad in the *Penny Pincher* she's been dancing around the room. She loves to sing. I like the idea of an all-girls choir."

"Actually," Mrs. Dunlap corrected me, "I have two choirs. The older girls perform as a group and the younger girls perform in a group. I also have them sing together at times. Katie would be a candidate for the junior group. Has Katie ever sung professionally?"

"No," I said, wincing a little. "But she is very enthusiastic. I can't sing so I really can't tell you about the quality of Katie's voice."

Mrs. Dunlap chuckled. "I like honest answers. I'd love to audition her. We audition on Wednesday evenings at the university's school of music. Can you bring her?"

A bit stunned, I said, "Sure. Which Wednesday?"

"How's a week from tomorrow at 7:30pm? Do you know where the university's school of music is located?"

"I do."

"Meet me in the piano lab. Can Katie read music?"

Now was a moment of pride. "Yes, she has taken clarinet lessons for three years at school."

Mrs. Dunlap's voice perked up. "I'm looking forward to meeting you and hearing Katie sing."

Katie was sitting on the living-room floor building a wood-block city, oblivious to her surroundings. "Hey kiddo," I said, nudging her. "I talked to Mrs. Dunlap."

Katie's eyes got as wide as harvest moons. "What did she say?"

"You have an audition date for AGTC next Wednesday at 7:30 at the university."

Katie leaped up, knocking over her architecture, the pieces flying. We both laughed and I gave her a giant hug. "How do I prepare?" Katie asked nervously.

"There is nothing to prepare for. I'll bring you to your audition. You'll sing for Mrs. Dunlap. And then we see what happens."

"Mom," she said, looking at me intently. "I really, really want this."

"I know sweetie. Let's just see what happens."

I had grave misgivings about this audition. I was absolutely certain that this organization was legitimate. What I wasn't sure of was if Katie was going to meet their expectations for membership. All I cared about was that my little girl, who had been through so much, not be hurt yet again. I really didn't care about the choir's quality, status, or reputation. I just wanted Katie to feel like she belonged somewhere. So, Katie and I both held our collective breaths for an entire week.

I pulled up to the portico of the school of music. All the lights were on and college students were milling around circulating in and out of the revolving glass doors at the entrance. I was looking for a place to park and on-street parking wasn't looking promising. I had 15 minutes to park. I started to panic. Just as I inched my way past the portico, a public parking garage appeared. "YES!" I exclaimed. I nabbed a spot, unbuckled my seat belt, and motioned to Katie to follow me. She was literally frozen in her seat. I leaned over to the passenger side, kissed her cheek, and said, "This is going to be fine." She leaned her head on my shoulder and unbuckled her belt. We held hands as we walked toward the school of music.

As Katie and I slipped through the revolving door, I asked one of the students where the piano lab was. She said, "Oh, you must be here for Mrs. Dunlap. Follow me." The door to the lab was open and there, sat at the piano, was a middle-aged woman singing with the most exquisite voice I had ever heard. I hated to interrupt her. I turned to Katie and she had hidden behind me. She was terrified. I knocked on the open door. The woman stopped playing, greeted me, and Katie peeked out from behind me to greet her. "I'm Mrs. Dunlap, Katie. I'm going to ask your mom to wait in the student lounge and you and I are going to sing." Katie let go of my hand. I suppressed the urge to give her one last hug, and then the door to the piano room closed. I weaved my way to the lounge. I hadn't brought anything to read so all I could do was chew on my lip and pray that Katie would get through this okay. *How long does an audition take? This seems a bit long. Maybe that's a good sign?* Finally, Mrs. Dunlap poked her head around the corner and asked me to come back. More prayers.

She began, "Katie has a delicate pitch-perfect voice. She needs some training but she has all the basics to make an outstanding singer. I'd like to work with her." I held back a gasp and thanked her repeatedly for her time and expertise. She turned to Katie and said, "Would you like to sing for AGTC, Katie?" My daughter was speechless but nodded her head furiously. Mrs. Dunlap laughed. "I think that was a yes."

"I guarantee you it was a yes," I said, with a chuckle.

Mrs. Dunlap handed me a very formidable packet of forms to be filled out. She asked me to mail the forms back to her as soon as possible along with her registration fee. Katie would begin singing with AGTC at the beginning of her sixth-grade school year.

It was a miracle that AGTC entered Katie's life at the same time Willow Wood Middle School did. Without a doubt, AGTC saved Katie that semester. It was her one place of refuge in a sea of hell.

Our seven-year relationship with AGTC had just begun.

I tucked a very excited Katie into bed that night. All she could talk about was AGTC. "I'm going to be a professional singer, Mom!" I hadn't really let that soak in. How could I be her mom all these years and not know she had this gift? I had missed something important about my daughter. It made me wonder what else I was missing. I began to pound myself into the ground, berating myself for not really knowing her.

I turned to her and said, "I'm very proud of you, Katie."

She sat straight up in bed and gave me a big hug. "Mom, I didn't know I could do this. I hoped, but I didn't know." I kissed her forehead and told her she was about to start a brand-new adventure. "What about Dad? What if he says no?"

I smiled at her. "We'll convince him!"

She fell back on her pillow, hugged White Bunny, and closed her eyes.

*

I sat at the kitchen table and read each sheet in the acceptance package one by one. There was every kind of form you could imagine, from basic name, address, phone number to permission to transport to permission to obtain medical care. There were instructions to make sure her health insurance covered away travel and a form for immunizations. There was a detailed medical form that had to be filled out by Daniel. There was a form asking for three emergency contacts. There was a liability document that I didn't understand. There was a 2001 performance schedule and a measurement size for her three uniforms. And, of course, there was the fee schedule. The numbers took my breath away. Finally, there was the agreement to perform with AGTC for the 2001–2002 school year and assume all financial liability. *I'm turning complete control over my daughter to an organization and people I don't even know*. Paranoia set in. I was trapped between Katie's happiness and my fear of losing say over her care while she was participating in this organization. There was no way I could enroll Katie in this organization without Joe's consent as well. In fact, all the documents required two parents' signatures. It was late, but I called Joe. I was sick to my stomach.

"Hello, this is Joe."

"Hi Joe, this is Tova."

"What's up?" he said flatly.

"I have amazing news. Katie auditioned for a well-known all-girl touring choir and was accepted."

"Oh. I didn't know she could sing."

"Yes, the director of the choir, Mrs. Dunlap, auditioned her this evening. She said Katie had a lovely, delicate voice and perfect pitch."

"Wow. Who'd have thought that?" I couldn't tell if he was being sarcastic or not.

Now for the hard part. "Mrs. Dunlap gave me a very complex acceptance packet that we both have to go through and sign. In fairness, Joe, this is a full-time commitment for all three of us and a huge financial obligation."

He got snitty. "You mean a financial obligation for me."

"Yes, for you." I sighed.

"How much?" When I quoted the tuition price, he said, "Well, before I say yes, I have news for you." I braced myself for one of Joe's nasty surprises. "I sold the house for cash."

I was stunned. "Katie never told me ..."

"I didn't tell her. I wasn't sure the deal would go through."

I didn't ask how much the house was sold for. It wasn't my business. I had long ago signed over my rights to that dreadful white elephant.

"So I have the resources to finance AGTC," he said. My jaw dropped. "But I have one request."

I was hardly in a position to say no, but I was suspicious. He went on. "I'd like to be the volunteering parent." *Huh?* "I like traveling. Katie should have one of us there given how anxious she gets. You are such a mess most of the time and I wouldn't want you embarrassing Katie."

Ah, there's the knife. "Joe, was that really necessary? I haven't had an admission in over two years. I'm not perfect but I'm not a mess."

He ignored me. "I can come over tomorrow and read the packet."

Holding my wound, I said, "I'll call Daniel and get the medical forms filled out."

We hung up, with the condemnation "You're a mess" reverberating in my head.

When Katie got home from school the next day, I sat her down and gave her the good news. "Your dad said yes to AGTC. And he's willing to pay the tuition. And guess what! Your dad wants to volunteer!"

Katie was silent for a second. "Does he have to volunteer and why does he want to?"

She asked good questions for which I had no answer. I said softly, "Give him a chance. Anyway, you are officially a member of AGTC! Let's celebrate! Your dad is coming over at 8pm but we have time for spaghetti."

Joe arrived at 9:30 for our 8pm meeting. *Some things never change*. It was Katie's bedtime but I let her stay up to greet her dad. Joe and I went through each page of the forms. He nitpicked. I tuned him out. All I wanted was his signature. When we completed the packet, he seemed satisfied. All I had to do was stop at Daniel's office and get the medical forms.

Joe turned to me. "Are you going to mail it?"

"Are you kidding? I'm hand-delivering this envelope."

Joe pulled out his checkbook and wrote the tuition check. I couldn't help but wonder if it would actually clear.

*

Mrs. Dunlap ran a tight ship. There were 30 girls aged eight to 18 and they traveled a lot. She was very particular about uniforms. For formal events, the younger girls wore long black skirts, white blouses, teal cummerbunds, and teal bow ties. The older girls wore long black gowns and white pearl necklaces. Girls with long hair had to wear it in a single French braid down their backs. For informal occasions, it was khaki shorts and matching T-shirts or khaki pants and red pullover tops. No jewelry, hair bows, or barrettes were allowed. Shoes for formal occasions had to be black pumps, and for informal performances, white canvas sneakers.

The list of rules was formidable.

However, the music these girls created was stunning. They sang at weddings, corporate parties, competitions all over the country, and the biannual children's choir competitions in Disney World. They had a Christmas and spring formal concert every year that was sometimes standing-room-only attended. Besides the performance fees, the organization had fundraisers, everything from art auctions to spaghetti dinners. Mrs. Dunlap was a miracle worker. Not just with the organization but also with Katie.

The combination of Northview School and AGTC transformed Katie from a bullied, fragile little girl to a confident pre-adolescent. Nothing helps a child more than to discover she's really good at something and have that something encouraged. I let Joe take the lead as a chaperone on tours. He got an ego rush from being the only dad in the traveling parent group. In the beginning, I tried to help with the fundraisers, carpool for rehearsals, and getting the girls ready for local performances. However, just like I never mastered the art of the French braid, I never mastered the art of integrating into the AGTC mother culture. These women were far above my social and emotional paygrade. We had no common ground. I consoled myself that at least I was good at finding the girls' lost shoes. It was a reflection of my self-worth. My specialty was lost items.

What held me back from being a fully-participating parent was my shame at my illness. Okay, maybe Joe's cutting comments did get to me. My confidence was low and he had a gift for shattering it. I slipped into a bipolar depression Katie's seventh-grade grade year. It was a long, drawn out illness that lasted several months and left me totally incapable of basic human interaction. Through Katie's first year at AGTC, I did my best to volunteer. During her next year, the sum total of my participation consisted of showing up for performances and suffering through mandatory fundraisers. Joe had made quite a name for himself as the dad chaperone and Mrs. Dunlap relied on him for many practical tasks. I was a ghost. Barely there, barely noticed. While I was never hospitalized, my depression significantly impaired my ability to fulfill basic life requirements. AGTC obligations were out of my reach. I didn't allow Katie to bring friends home. I believed Joe's words that I would embarrass her as she developed social relationships. She spent more time with her dad since he was the AGTC parent and had the more desirable living arrangement. I spent a lot of time alone, hating myself.

Katie entered AGTC at the beginning of sixth grade and participated until her junior year in high school. AGTC was the glue that held Katie's world together.

*

Northview School was a watershed period of time for Katie. Besides starting AGTC, she sprouted up academically.

Elizabeth, her teacher, called me into her tiny and cluttered office one day. "I'm puzzled by something," she began. "Katie is clearly gifted. Her ability to absorb new information, think creatively, problem solve, and read far above grade level makes me wonder why she is stuck in third-grade math and science."

I gave Elizabeth the complete story of Katie's experiences at the Willow Wood School District. Elizabeth nodded. "She's too traumatized to move forward," she said.

I was stunned. Only Katie's therapists understood that.

Elizabeth said, "I want to work with Katie one-on-one and see just how far I can get her to progress. I'll give you updates."

I was so grateful. Katie finally had a teacher who believed in her. And Elizabeth was true to her word. She coaxed Katie and Katie responded by devouring her math books. One grade level at a time, Katie whizzed through the material.

I got a call from Elizabeth. "Tova, I want you to know that in six months Katie has gone from not being able to multiply to doing algebra. I've never seen anything like it. Willow Wood should be ashamed of itself."

"You're a miracle worker," I said.

"No, I just gave Katie a chance to reclaim her math. The rest was all her doing."

I hung up the phone and absorbed just how fast my little songbird had progressed, emotionally, academically, and talent-wise. I could never have imagined just five years earlier that the terrified first grader I had to uproot from chaos would blossom so gorgeously.

*

From 1996 when I took Katie's hand and escorted her out of Joe's chaotic world, till 2002 when Katie entered Northview School, my total focus was on repairing the damage I had done to my daughter through my abandoning of her during my illnesses.

Now, at this new juncture in our lives, it was time for me to turn inward. I was not done healing. In many ways, I put my own work on hold to help my daughter find her footing in the world. With the careful prescribing and patient ear of Dr. Guterson, I had managed to avoid a hospitalization throughout Katie's fifth- and sixth-grade years. However, the fact that I hadn't completely unraveled in those years didn't mean I wasn't still in desperate pain and tortured by childhood memories I couldn't escape. I remember the day I walked into his office and announced, "Katie's future doesn't have to be my present."

"What do you mean?" he asked.

"She's not broken and I still am."

He looked at me with a kind of sadness that I rarely saw in him. "No, she's not broken and one day soon you won't feel broken either."

"I'm not my caregivers?"

"You are absolutely not your caregivers." I almost believed him. He asked, "What do you want for you that doesn't have something to do with Katie?"

The thought that I had a choice shocked me. The truth was, I didn't know. I looked up at him and said as much. "I don't know where I'm going. As Katie's and my paths diverge more and more, I feel left behind. She's growing. She's conquering her obstacles and I'm still living events of 1965. It'll never end."

He said, "Let's take this journey in baby steps. Right now, give some thought to what you want in your future. Play with the idea."

I looked at him, puzzled. "I have a future?"

"Yes, you do, and a bright one."

It occurred to me that the less Katie's life paralleled mine, the easier the job of parenting was getting. I wasn't parenting Katie and me anymore. I was now just parenting Katie. I felt Atlas's weight lifted from my shoulders.

*

Joe, Katie, and I sat across from each other. The topic: high school.

Katie had entered eighth grade at Northview and it was time for the three of us to decide what to do about freshman year. I wanted another private school, similar to Northview. I still saw Katie as needing a protective environment. Joe wanted a public school where Katie would have more academic options (and he didn't have to pay tuition).

Katie had an idea neither of us expected. She wanted to go to the city's creative and performing arts high school, otherwise known as CAPA. I panicked. It was only three short years ago that she was nearly ripped to shreds by a public-school system that was supposed to be the best in the state. I couldn't imagine how she'd survive in an urban public school. Her idea sounded like a recipe for disaster.

However, her new therapist, Tom, told me emphatically that Katie was 14 years old and as long as her idea wasn't completely unreasonable, she should try out what she wanted. We received the CAPA application packet in the mail and Katie very carefully, with Mrs. Dunlap's help, filled it out. I never thought the application would get very far. I was humoring Tom and Katie. When Katie's audition date arrived in the mail, it started to look more serious.

The day of the audition I drove Katie to CAPA. Never having been there, I had to confess the building was new and impressive. We took the stairs to the vocal department. There was a row of chairs outside the audition room. Waiting as well was a young girl next in line for her audition. She and Katie struck up a conversation and Katie was oblivious to my presence. This gave me time to explore the floor.

First thing I did was check out the bathroom to see if it was in good working order. I was stunned to discover it was pristine. I was puzzled at how a high-school bathroom could be that clean. I was warming up to this building. The young woman ahead of Katie was called in for her audition. Katie wished her good luck and the girl said, "You too."

And that might have been the last they saw of each other, if it wasn't for a turn of events that would bring them both back together in a most unusual place, participants at a camp for blind children. The pairing would bring out the best in my daughter.

Memories of Katie's AGTC audition played in my head. She was so scared, so fragile, and I ached for her. Fast forward to 2004, she thumbed through her music and hummed her part, completely engaged and mature. As I watched my daughter, I realized I had misjudged her. Maybe CAPA was the perfect school for her. Now I was actually hoping for an acceptance.

Katie was called in. I could hear her through the door. I sat in stunned silence. *Oh my, she really can sing.*

It was my first actual awareness of just how talented my daughter was. I had been told, but I hadn't really understood it wholly.

Katie came out smiling. The person holding the auditions said we'd get a letter in about a month. Katie's letter came in two weeks. She was going to CAPA. *Note to self: trust your daughter.* We later learned that a vocal admission was the hardest one to get. I was told everyone thinks they can sing and few actually can. Katie was amongst the few, not the many. I was proud of her.

CAPA turned out to be nothing like I expected. It was a high school filled with Katies, some with blue hair expertly playing the oboe, some with nose piercings who wrote exquisite poetry, others in yarmulkes lugging around enormous cellos, and some in tights pirouetting down the halls. Katie truly was at home in this school. In four years of CAPA, Katie was never bullied once. She had a circle of friends that do what creative teenagers do (like dying their cat's paws green for St. Patrick's Day). I liked all her friends and Katie exuded happiness the entire time she was there.

I attended Katie's freshman recital. She sang an Italian aria, a piece from Gilbert and Sullivan, and a playful dance melody from the sixteenth century. I cried throughout the whole thing. How did the little girl who sat in chilly bath water singing songs from *The Little Mermaid* grow up to sing opera? In that second, I loved her with all the fierceness my fear and illness didn't allow me when she was an infant. Not only had Katie come full circle, so had I.

CHAPTER 13

LAST RAINBOW

I thought I had this parenting thing nailed. She was 15, doing extremely well in school, had a gift she loved to explore, and a close-knit circle of friends.

As for me, I had very few relapses, and I was making plans to return to the workforce full-time. After nine years of really hard work by both Katie and me, I was feeling pretty good about where I was heading and where Katie was heading.

However, sometimes life doesn't let us become comfortable.

It started with a scream of pain in the middle of the night. Katie had been experiencing severe headaches that we assumed were just migraines. As we bounced from neurologist to neurologist trying to get her relief, it became clear something was seriously wrong. Then she started to lose her vision. She lost not just acuity but also color vision as well.

The first months of her freshman year were preoccupied with a desperate attempt to find out what was medically wrong with my daughter.

The first tentative diagnosis was a brain tumor. After all the MRIs and CT scans, that terrifying option was ruled out. Then the physicians on her team started to explore more uncommon explanations. The next diagnosis they jumped to was an eye migraine. However, as her pain and vision loss remained despite aggressive treatment, that option was ruled out too. Finally, in the winter of 2005, Katie was diagnosed with intercranial hypertension (IH). It's a neurological condition caused by extremely high fluid pressure in the brain and it results in migraine-type headaches and blindness. IH is almost unheard of in children. Diagnosing the condition was a process of elimination and a lumbar puncture to measure her fluid pressure. The suspicion of IH was confirmed. By the time she was diagnosed, some of the damage to her eyes would be permanent. In the middle of nineth grade, Katie was diagnosed as both legally blind and color blind.

It all happened so quickly. Just like when she was a newborn and we were facing the possibility of meningitis, I reverted back into my crisis management skills. I navigated a complex medical situation as best I could. One referral after another, one test after another, I shepherded my songbird through the system. Joe helped as much as he could, but I was the parent who wasn't working full-time. A lot of the immediate decisions fell to me.

I felt powerless.

Every night, Katie screamed in pain begging me to make it stop. Every day, I was on the phone with yet another physician's office pushing for an appointment or a test. Daniel was great. He helped us break the log-jam of long waits and contradictory medical opinions. I didn't have the luxury of taking time to tally how I was doing psychiatrically. Dr. Guterson saw me frequently, adjusted my medications appropriately, and kept me out of the hospital. I just kept pushing forward until someone could explain to me why my teenage daughter couldn't match the colors of her clothes anymore. The diagnosis of IH was a relief. Katie's second ophthalmologist finally solved the puzzle. He ordered a lumbar puncture and Katie's fluid pressure was extremely high. The tell-tale sign of IH. Once we navigated the diagnosis, it was time to tackle management.

IH took a terrible toll on Katie. She was in excruciating pain most of the time. Her headaches were incapacitating and she missed a lot of school because of them. I remember often being awoken by the sound of Katie's voice begging me to make the pain stop. She would literally crawl into my room unable to lift her head. I would get us both dressed as quickly as I could and race to the emergency room used by the eye hospital. The staff, knowing her, took her right back, set up an IV with pain medication and performed a spinal tap. A spinal tap is the go-to procedure to drain fluid and relieve pressure on the optic nerves and brain. Katie got relief. After a five-hour emergency room treatment, I piled my exhausted child into the car and took her home.

This scene repeated itself over and over again.

Once she had been diagnosed, we had to manage the illness. Managing pain in a child is a tricky. Even with a diagnosis as obviously pain-inducing as IH, getting treatment for it was an uphill battle. Katie and I made an appointment with Daniel to specifically discuss pain management. There had been no good answer up until that point. We couldn't keep going to the ER. There had to be something we could do at home to make the suffering bearable for her. Daniel presented us with several options but with Joe's history of narcotic addiction, he was cautious about what to prescribe her. We decided she would try a new non-narcotic pain medication. We didn't know if it would help, but we had few options. As it turned out, the new drug did give her some relief. Added to her IH medications, it was the best medical science could offer her. At least, that meant fewer ER visits and less time missed from school.

ERs and Daniel were just part of Katie's medical team. We also had her ophthalmologist, Dr. Roberts. I remember our first appointment with him. I sat in Dr. Roberts waiting room with Katie. He was Katie's fourth ophthalmologist. I wanted a better answer than "She'd need to learn to adjust". I wanted the diagnosis reversed completely. I wanted someone to tell me, "I have great news for you, Ms. Feinman, Katie was misdiagnosed. She'll be just fine." That was not Dr. Roberts diagnosis. He talked about white canes, learning braille, adaptive technology, and receiving special education services for her visual impairment. He was gentle with us. Dr. Roberts was an older man who had seen a lot of eyes in his long career. In a subtle way, he was telling me to accept Katie's diagnosis and her impairment. It was time for me to move from fighting to acceptance because if I didn't, Katie never would.

Katie had a mixed reaction toward her blindness. On one hand, she was completely open to learning everything and anything she needed to learn to adapt to her condition. On the other hand, she was resentful and uncooperative at home. I understood the dichotomy. Katie was resilient. If learning braille and how to use a white cane were the path toward her freedom to read and navigate, Katie was all in. However, at home, even the simplest requests were met with a wall of resistance. I'd ask her to feed Frodo and she'd reply, "I'm blind. I can't." I'd ask her to help with the dishes. She'd sullenly reply, "I'm blind. I can't." Also, she was so angry all the time. A combination of constant pain and losing her sight, especially losing her ability to read print, enraged her. She often took that rage out on me and I felt helpless to respond. I didn't know if I was supposed to be firm with her, nurturing to her, or give in to her. Just like in years past, I needed help to navigate this new earthquake in Katie's life. I turned to Mrs. Ryan, Katie's special-ed vision instructor. She met me for lunch in the middle of the school day. An act of kindness for which I will be eternally grateful.

I sat across from Mrs. Ryan at local coffee shop. I started the conversation. "Marie, I don't know how to help her. She's angry all the time and resentful of even the smallest of requests. She's been through so much in her life and this is just cruel. I want to wrap her in bubble wrap and keep her from every possible harm she no longer can see. If I could take the pain of her headaches on myself, I would gladly."

Marie listened to me thoughtfully and responded, "I have students who have been completely blind from birth to students, like Katie, who have become visually impaired later in childhood. I tell all my parents the same thing. Force independence, as much as is reasonable for the child's age and mobility skill level. If you give in to your protective instincts, you will cripple her. She has a lot of potential. She'll need some skills, but she can live a full and productive life if you don't paralyze her."

I pondered Marie's words and replied, "I don't pity her. I'm furious that she, just as her life was coming together, was forced to deal with this. I want to fight her battles for her because the injustice is too hard for me to bear."

"Your anger is natural but it will ruin her chances at a completely mobile life. I know I'm asking the near impossible, but fight your mother-instinct, for her sake."

I could see the profound wisdom in what Marie was sharing. She didn't know Katie's and my history so I couldn't explain to her why I felt so overwhelmingly controlled by my instinct to protect. This was a conversation left to Dr. Guterson.

I shifted the topic. "What skills is Katie learning and how can I help?"

Marie switched gears and clicked into teacher mode. "Right now, I'm teaching her white cane skills, navigating city streets safely, and braille. Katie is a braille whizz. She's really bright."

"Yeah, she's gifted in many ways. She has a passion for reading. I know braille will be her single-minded focus."

Marie reassured me, "She will use those gifts to cope with her vision impairment as well. Don't baby her. She can do this. Don't get in her way. That's how you can help."

Marie had given me a lot to think about. We parted with a promise to keep in touch.

I sat in the coffee shop long after Marie had departed. She gave me my marching orders, now I needed a plan. I always felt better about complex problems when I had a plan of action. First thing on the list was to call Katie's therapist. Tom had been working with Katie for about two years. Not since Laurie had I witnessed Katie bond so well with a psychologist. Tom understood adolescents and knew exactly how to talk to Katie to get positive results. I told Tom what Marie had said and he agreed completely. He cautioned me to not play therapist and stick to my role as her mother. That stung a bit because I was so accustomed to digging into the psychology of every problem, either mine or Katie's. Tom softened. "I've got the therapy thing covered. You focus on keeping her life as normal as possible." I hung up feeling a bit less terrified. Katie had a team. She was not alone with her visual impairment and blinding pain, and neither was I.

Returning to life under new normal, Katie's 16th birthday was fast approaching. I had literally been saving for this birthday for almost three years once I started a part-time research job. I wanted to treat her to the most indulgent 16th birthday I could create. I started by making reservations at a highly recommended upscale restaurant. I then ordered symphony tickets in the desirable "orchestra circle". Even if Katie couldn't see the orchestra, she'd be in the perfect location for the best sound experience. Next, I reserved transport to escort us to all our destinations and then home. The cherry on the top of this blow-out birthday bash was a trip the following day to the animal shelter. I had gotten long sought-after permission from my landlord to adopt a cat. Katie would finally get her long-desired kitty. I kept that information a secret for so long, I thought I was going to explode with it. We'd drive to the shelter under the guise that Teresa wanted a new cat. When we got there, it would be Katie picking out a cat. I was so excited I could barely contain myself. I may have been missing in action for Katie's fourth birthday, but I was absolutely going to be there for her 16th birthday.

Her big day arrived and we dressed up like we were going to a wedding. Our escort was on time. It was drizzling but the weather didn't dampen the moment. We had reservations at the restaurant at 5pm. We were exactly on time. We were dropped off like royalty. I guided Katie into the restaurant and around obstacles. The host greeted us, asked us about our reservation, and led us straight back to our table. The linen table cloth, napkins, china, and crystal were all laid out in splendor. The truly magnificent part of our seating was the glass windows that spanned the entire length of the restaurant. We were given front-row seats to the spectacular city skyline. Katie could vaguely make out some features through the window and was thrilled for what little of the view she could see. The menus arrived. I read Katie her menu and we made our selections, patiently waiting for the waiter to return and take our orders. We chatted about her friends, CAPA, and AGTC, amongst other topics. The vibe between us was warm.

Katie fell silent and gazed out the window. I caught a glimpse of a rainbow just within view. I pointed the rainbow out to Katie and asked if she could see it. She was quiet for a minute and answered, "I can see it. Mom. A rainbow for my 16th birthday."

I teased. "I arranged for it with G-d."

She looked at me and, with a winsome tone, asked, "Do you think this will be the last rainbow I ever see?"

I wanted so desperately to tell her no, that she would see somehow, that maybe a cure would come, that we could pray about it. I didn't. I simply said, "Then capture this rainbow in your memory so you have it forever."

In our perfect Symphony Hall seats, we listened to our internationally recognized orchestra play Gustav Holst's "The Planets". It's a beautiful set of suites that literally swept you off your feet and carried you into the solar system. However, I was still at the restaurant, staring at the rainbow. It was hard to break away from the image of what might have been Katie's last rainbow. As my mind drifted in time with the music, I was brought back to an event in 1998. Joe had given Katie a telescope for her eighth birthday. She was overjoyed with her gift and insisted we use it immediately. I took her to the side of a soccer field which was clear of trees and pitch dark. The city lights were behind us so we had an unencumbered view of the night sky. I knew nothing about telescopes, but between us, we figured out how to position it and view through it. There, in the front of the scope, was the planet Mars. Katie squealed with delight. Her goal was to see all eight planets. She understood that Neptune, Uranus, and Pluto were out of reach but she was sure if she got the coordinates right, we could see Saturn. I don't know if we ever actually caught a glimpse of Saturn but for me that wasn't the point. Katie and I were connecting over the heavenly bodies in the sky.

My attention returned to the symphony and sure enough, the segment was "Mars". I looked over at Katie, enthralled with the music and struggling to read her program. I leaned my head onto hers and she leaned back. The symphony played on, oblivious to the power of the moment for a mother and her blind daughter in the audience.

The evening was over and our escort dropped us off in front of our house. Katie and I were tired but happy as well. It was a stunning way to spend her 16th birthday. The next day she was to get her mystery gift. I told her we were picking Teresa up first because she wanted to go to the animal shelter. Katie answered, "While we're there, can I pick out a cat?"

Stifling a giggle, I told her a cat for her would be very difficult to arrange. She pouted. We picked up Teresa and all Katie wanted to do was convince me to get her a cat. Teresa and I smiled knowingly at each other. We arrived at the animal shelter and Katie sulked.

I asked, "Do you want to come in?"

She sullenly answered, "Only if I can get a cat."

She's making this deliciously entertaining.

165

Teresa coaxed her out of the car with a promise to let her pick out the cat. She grudgingly went along with the plan. We went into the kennel, turned to the first cage, first shelf, and there was a calico one-year-old cat named Rosebud. Katie put her hand up to the grate and Rosebud put up her paw. Katie exclaimed, "This kitty is perfect, Teresa!" Teresa urged Katie to play with the kitty a bit and see if she was friendly. Rosebud rubbed all over Katie, purred, and eventually jumped in her lap. I couldn't hold back any longer. I said, "Rosebud is actually your cat."

Katie looked at me, mouth agape. "Mine?"

"Yours."

I got my hug as the shelter personnel prepared the paperwork and carrier for Rosebud. Katie finally had her cat. Our list of adopted species was complete. I bought a sweatshirt for her that read, "Books and Cats … Life is Good." It became her comfort shirt.

Not long after the birthday bash, I got a phone call from Marie. She wanted to enroll Katie in blind camp for the summer. She explained to me that the purpose of the camp was to teach blind students life skills. She said they would learn everything from basic cooking techniques to how to put on eye make-up.

I agreed that the camp sounded like a good idea and that I'd talk to Joe and get his permission as well. Joe agreed to it. Katie was signed up for six-week overnight camp at the Blind and Vision Institute. I dropped her off with her belongings. We met the house mother, and she gave me a tour of the facilities. The bedrooms were dormitory style and the activity rooms were on the first floor. I saw the computer rooms, the kitchen, the sewing room, the laundry area, as well as classrooms and a library with braille and large print books. It was clear that Katie was in good hands. However, Katie was less than thrilled about the accommodation. She had done overnights many times on tour with AGTC so I knew that wasn't the problem. I speculated that it was because this was a life skills lesson camp. She was none too happy with the itinerary and the fact that she had to get up at 7am every morning. My Sleeping Beauty preferred 10am. Ah well, she needed to be here and she'd adjust. I left knowing she was in good hands.

Two days into camp, I got a call from Katie. The call began with, "I'm in prison."

I stifled a laugh. "No, honey, if this were a prison, it's the most luxurious and expensive prison I've ever heard of."

When that complaint didn't work, she tried, "I hate the food. It's old-people food."

"What do you mean by "old-people food"?"

She whined, "They serve mashed potatoes and applesauce."

"You like apple sauce and mashed potatoes."

Then came the obligatory, "Mom, you aren't listening to me."

I patiently replied, "Yes Katie, I am listening to you. You are in a very nice place and they are serving you food you like."

She became petulant. "They serve me pork. I tell them I can't eat it but they serve it anyway."

She got me there. This was a problem. We may not have begun keeping kosher yet but we didn't eat pork. "You make a valid point; I'll fix the pork problem."

She responded, annoyed, "Fine. If that's all you'll do for me, I'll take it."

I told her I loved her and she should try to enjoy camp. She slammed down the phone and I laughed out loud.

During the course of six weeks, I got a number of calls from the house mother about how Katie was trying to stage a rebellion against the sleeping arrangements, the food, and the outdoor recreation. It seems she and Ronna, a friend of hers from CAPA, found themselves at the same blind camp together and wanted to be roommates. Fortunately, each of them had a roommate who also preferred different sleeping arrangements. When Ronna and Katie couldn't get staff to rearrange the room assignments, Katie and Ronna did it on their own. I apologized to the house mother and offered to drive over and talk to Katie. The house mother chuckled. "No, she's fine. Katie has spunk. A lot of our children are too afraid to challenge rules. Katie isn't being rude. She's standing up for what she thinks is right. I just wanted you to know."

My compliant child had struck a blow for independence.

The last week in camp the students were taken to an outdoor campground for swimming, rope climbing, canoeing, goal ball (a game played with a beeping ball), and archery. I pondered the wisdom of letting 15 blind children shoot bows and arrows. I calmed myself with the knowledge that every year they take students to this camp and every year all the kids make it back alive. When I picked Katie up from camp, she was all smiles. She had to admit that blind camp was not so bad. It also had some amazing effects. She made her bed, started wearing make-up, baked me chocolate chip cookies, and expressed an interest in sewing her own clothes. *Who are you and what did you do to my child?* However, as I got used to the more independent Katie, I was pretty impressed with what the camp was able to teach her in six short weeks.

My daughter had once again found her footing. Just like she did in sixth grade moving from Willow Wood to Northview School, she faced tremendous hardship and emerged victorious. It took an entire team to help her make light out of darkness. Dr. Roberts, her ophthalmologist, Marie, her vision and mobility instructor, Tom, her psychotherapist, Daniel, her pediatrician, the staff at CAPA High School, and Rachel Dunlap. Mrs. Dunlap was remarkable with Katie. She was empathetic toward Katie's vision loss but she she was in no way willing to indulge it. Mrs. Dunlap was better at making Katie be independent than I was.

She was straightforward. First, she told Katie what the task was going to be and then she asked her what she would need to accomplish the task. She took into account Katie's needs and fostered her confidence. Mrs. Dunlap pulled me aside one day and told me Katie was her hero. This from a no-nonsense woman who shepherded 30 girls all around the country singing while she herself battled breast cancer. Mrs. Dunlap was my hero.

As high school was drawing to a close, Katie wanted to add one more member to her support team. A Seeing Eye dog named Cloud. We were narrowing our choices for college down and asking for accommodations for a guide dog hadn't figured in the plan. I began to worry. How was a dog going to manage living in a dorm room? How was Katie going to meet the dog's needs? How would the dog be received by her dormmates? Was Katie mature enough for the responsibility of caring for such a specialized dog by herself?

In order to answer my questions, I did what I had done for the past four years of Katie's high-school term. I turned to Marie. Marie said, "Of all my students, I believe Katie is most capable of using a guide dog effectively. Don't worry about colleges accommodating the two of them. They legally have to meet Katie's needs." With Marie's reassurance, Katie registered to attend guide-dog school in order to get matched and trained with her four-legged furry set of new eyes.

No parent, mentally ill or not, ever imagines facing blindness in their child. While Katie was surrounded with the most amazing support team for her needs, I relied on Dr. Guterson for my needs. In his office, I cried my grief, my guilt, and my fears. I remember his sage words. "In this room, you can cry or be any way you want to be. In front of Katie, you need to be her mom."

I did exactly what he prescribed. Was there guilt? You bet. After what her early childhood had been like, it made me sick that she had to endure this trial just as her future was so bright. I wept for all the things Katie would not be able to see in the future:

smiles, books, stars, and rainbows came to mind. Was there grief and fear? Absolutely. I didn't know what kind of future my gifted and blind daughter might face. I worried about how she'd be limited. She wanted to study math in college. Could she do that now? She wanted to travel abroad for a semester. I wondered if that dream was out of reach for her. Later in life, she wanted to marry and have children. Was that dream still possible? Every parent has dreams for their child. I always imagined Katie as a math professor at some small elite liberal arts school. I pictured her singing solos in the community choir. I imagined her married to a nerdy Jewish man and raising their children. My imagination held a thousand possible futures for her, but none of them included blindness.

Dr. Guterson helped me navigate treacherous waters.

Katie's physical pain and pleas for help plunged me into a kind of empathy that made it difficult for me to separate her pain from mine. Sometimes, I was so traumatized by all the physician's offices and ERs I had to fight my way through that I felt more like an abused child than Katie's mom. I had a long-tortured history with callous MDs. The ones that treated my injuries but let their causes go unaddressed. The ones that could not look me in the eye as they addressed my wounds. While I learned to stand up for my daughter's needs with her dad, the medical establishment, and educational system, I really didn't get much better at standing up for my own needs. I fought because Katie needed me to. My demons lived just beneath the surface, as I faked adulthood in encounters with Joe, physicians, insurance companies, teachers, and mental health professionals. My decisive battles, yet to come, would play out after Katie left home and I was on my own. My job was to help my daughter battle her life's challenge. Mine, would have to wait a little while longer to be addressed.

Long ago, Carrie said I wasn't ready to confront my demons. I knew that time would come when Katie was safely an adult. For now, this was Katie's moment.

Katie would blaze her own trail, armed with her talents, gifts, braille skills, and soon-to-be guide dog, Cloud. I didn't have to rework my imagination. Katie's was enough for both of us. I would simply follow her lead, celebrate every accomplishment and commiserate about every set-back. Blind or sighted, Katie would make her own way. She was fearless.

CHAPTER 14

GRADUATION

As I watched Katie cross the stage with her sighted guide in her white graduation gown to receive her diploma from CAPA High School, I wept. Not the tears I shed 18 years prior when post-partum depression was beginning to grip me, but tears of joy. She, in spite of overwhelming obstacles, came to this moment, victorious. However, I wasn't thinking about her future at that moment. I was scanning our past.

My therapist, Nancy, made a profoundly hopeful statement to me when I was in the throws of yet another round of shame for yet another relapse. She said, "Tova, children don't need perfect parents. They just need good enough parents." As I sat in the auditorium of Freedom Hall trying to drown out, with my thoughts, an overly politicized keynote speech, I created a panorama of the past 18 years in my mind.

Had I been good enough?

I broached the subject with Dr. Guterson once. He looked at me pensively and replied, "No one gets through childhood unscathed and no child could have had a mom who worked harder to make a good life for her. How Katie will ultimately resolve her inevitable conflicts with you, we'll have to wait and see. However, you did the best job you could do with the nearly impossible hand you were dealt. That matters and one day, it will matter to Katie as well."

I could make a long list of my failures as a mom, punish myself for them, and forever seek forgiveness I'd never accept. As I watched Katie cross the threshold into adulthood, I could either wallow in all that I failed at or I could celebrate that she and I made it this far. In truth, the best judge of my mothering was not going to be my opinion or even Katie's opinion. The best judge would be the actions she took in her future and how she handled her life's challenges. If the way she handled her blindness was any indication of future outcomes, I was sure my daughter would do just fine. Besides, I probably would never know if any challenge in her adult life was the result of something I had done (or not done) or something her dad had done. Katie was a hybrid of Joe, me, and her own uniqueness. It was pointless to wallow in the failures of the past because her future was now ultimately in her hands. The self-flagellation needed to draw to an end. That would take time, but I had Dr. Guterson. The day when I ended my own punishment would arrive. I just couldn't see that moment in my present.

I'll never know if I was a "good enough" mom. I do know, despite a brutal start, I loved Katie with a fierceness that I'm sure all mothers who were "good enough" felt. I wondered about all those other moms. Did they face mental illness, an abusive husband, a mental health system that gave up on them, poverty, bullying, and blindness? I wondered about the challenges all those "good enough" moms faced. I wasn't pitying myself. I was taking stock of Katie's and my journey. I asked the existential question.

Does a "good enough mom" ever feel that she is, in fact, *"good enough"*?

The speaker finally sat down, and the CAPA choir began singing. There in the upper-right side of the risers, three singers in, was my songbird. She was soon off to get her guide dog and when she returned, we'd frantically prepare for the college she had selected to attend in the fall. She decided on a small all-women's liberal arts college close to home. It had the best disabilities office of all the colleges she was accepted at and had a good academic program. Her plan was to major in education and math. I thought of mailing Willow Wood School District a copy of her transcript and telling them she's majoring in math. Okay, I'll admit, that was a little petty. I told Katie she should send her class schedule to Willow Wood. She laughed; "I really should."

As Joe and I exited the hall, looking for our daughter, I turned to him and said, "Did you ever think this day would come?"

"Yes," he said. "Katie can do anything."

I spontaneously hugged him. Joe was speechless. For me, that was a victory. Katie's friend led her to us. She was radiant. Joe hugged her. I hugged her. The three of us were off to Katie's favorite Italian restaurant. We were, after all these years, going to have family time.

As I watched her talk to her friend about college, I told myself it was finally time to let my baby bunny go.

ACKNOWLEDGEMENTS

I owe a profound debt of gratitude to Katie's pediatrician, Daniel Wolmark, MD, healer, and mentor. He set my feet on the path of healing when I was destroyed by post-partum depression. He shepherded Katie through a childhood of illnesses with skill and compassion. He was there for both Katie and me when she lost her sight. He became Katie's mentor well into her adulthood. His passing has left a hole in our family and especially in Katie's heart.

To my therapist Carrie, you took a broken human being and gave her a future she thought was unreachable. You single-handedly rescued me from a state hospital confinement and taught me how to fulfill my singular dream: reuniting with Katie as a family.

Yaakov Guterson, MD entered my life as my psychiatrist in 1995, the same time Katie reentered my life. He has been the integral source of my healing and my parenting for going on 24 years. He is the one person who has lived this story with me from the inside, from the moment Katie and I were reunited as a family to the present. Without him, *I'll Be Right Back* could not have happened.

Every child psychologist, starting with Dr. Laurie Davis, who I entrusted to nurture, support, and heal Katie and teach me to be a mom. Their wisdom and input spanned Katie's entire childhood and gave me the expert insight to parent. I could not have been a mom without their wise counsel, sensitivity, patience, and sometimes tough love.

Mrs. Rachel Dunlap heard a songbird in Katie's voice at a time in her life when Katie desperately needed to be heard. Mrs. Dunlap gifted Katie self-confidence and helped her tap into her natural gift for song. Rachel never got to see Katie graduate from high school or win a vocal scholarship in college. She lost her battle with cancer far too young. Every girl she trained still carries a piece of her in their hearts and in their song.

In 2005 Katie lost her sight. Mrs. Marie Ryan, Katie's Vision and Mobility instructor, took me under her wing and counseled me on how to handle the complex parenting of a legally blind child. Marie gave Katie back her independence and her joy of reading. She gave me the skills to help Katie thrive in life visually impaired.

Finally, I have a special place in my heart for every cluster of bunnies that made appearances in my life at miraculous times. Watching these gentle creatures nibble on dandelions as a family bridged a delicate moment between Katie and I and helped me find serenity in times when my life had none. I am a bunny mom and Katie will always be my baby bunny.

Now see Tova's story from another side ...

Extract from
Teacup in a Storm

CHAPTER 1

LIFE BEFORE DR. GUTERSON:

My story

I was a determined six-year-old, dangling precariously over the edge of a garbage dumpster behind my elementary school. I drooled, staring at the feast that lay just beyond my grasp. There was pudding, peanut butter and jelly sandwiches, peas, hamburgers, and brownies all laid out in front of me. All I needed was another foot of reach and the delicacies would be all mine. I had stopped feeling the hunger pangs in my stomach, but I couldn't get my brain to stop thinking about food. As I squirmed upside-down for a better reach, I heard a shout.

'Tova! What are you doing? Get out of there, you dirty girl!'

But I didn't want to get out of there.

I wanted pudding, but Mrs. Cooper was a frightening first-grade teacher. I tried to right myself as I pulled out of the dumpster, but instead I fell to the ground, my threadbare green plaid dress raised and exposing the previous night's shame. Mrs. Cooper glared at me and ordered me to stand up and turn around. Terrified, I tried to pull down my dress but the fabric got stuck in my underwear.

'Turn around, Tova, NOW!' the desiccated old woman bellowed.

I had no choice. I turned around, bare legs and buttocks exposed. Mrs. Cooper abruptly stopped screaming at me. As I quaked before her, she asked, 'How did you get hurt like that?'

I was truly baffled and said, 'I'm not hurt.'

Mrs. Cooper was incredulous. 'You are lying. Your legs and your bum are covered in welts and bruises. So, how did you get hurt?'

Rooting around for my courage, I turned and screamed, 'I'm not hurt! I don't get hurt, ever!'

The recess bell rang. I gave my dress one last yank, pulled up my stained knee socks, and ran to stand in line with the other children. Mrs. Cooper stared in disbelief as I whizzed past her, desperate to avoid her scrutiny.

*

As a child, I subsisted on a diet of trauma and terror, washing the bitter mixture down with my daily tears. My very existence depended on the decisions my stable of caregivers made for me, but that sacred trust was routinely violated. In the battle against their own psychological demons, they left me without protection, nurturance, and safety. The chaos of a childhood dominated by other people's untreated mental illnesses left me defenseless.

In the kaleidoscope world where reality was contorted by the psychoses of others – and where there was no safe space to find refuge – I clung to my only two childhood assets: my intellect and my innate certainty that G-d protected little girls. I used my intellect to create, in the safety of my own mind, a protected inner world to dwell in. That world was made up of the families I watched, with rapt attention, on the television programs that dominated the 1960s and 1970s. I relied on G-d for comfort when the brutality of the adult world intruded on my sanctuary. Early in my life, the Sabbath candle was my bridge to G-d.

I remember very vividly my first Shabbos, and the lifelong impact it would have on me. Stella, frail and world weary, stood before her silver candlesticks that Friday evening, waiting for 6.18pm. That time was just before the sun tucked below the horizon, and it signaled the beginning of Shabbos.

She struck a match at the sacred moment and, with an aura of reverence, lit all seven of her candles, one for every one of her children, living and deceased. The room flooded with light. The sweeping, circular motion of her gnarled hands mesmerized me as I leaned my bruised body into her fragile one. I listened in rapt attention as she sang a blessing in a language I did not understand but felt connected to somehow. The old woman took my tiny hand and whispered tenderly, 'Come sit with me, Tova.'

Battered but obedient, I cuddled up next to her. I stared at the flames rising up from the candles. Even at such a young age, I believed they were reaching for somewhere, some place mystical and sublime. The warmth emanating from the glow of the burning wicks was a holy warmth that melted away my suffering, at least in that moment, and beckoned me to snuggle, all the more, into Stella's frame. The woman turned to me, kissed my forehead, and softly said, 'Tova, G-d protects little girls.'

As I soaked in the holiness of the light, there was absolutely no doubt in my spiritually awakening mind that G-d did – and would indeed – protect me. I was a terrorized child with no human to turn to, but I found, in the light of Shabbos, a protector greater than any human guardian.

And I was right. G-d did come through for me. He gave me academic gifts and my inner safe space.

*

Years ago, I found this teacher's note while I was rummaging through a storage shed looking for a book to pack for college. It read:

To Whom It May Concern,

Tova is an extremely bright child. However, she has become quite a disruption in class. She stares out the window for long periods of time, totally unaware of where she is or what she is supposed to be learning. She has become the target of other students' nonstop teasing and yet shows no reaction to it. She is in danger of failing all her subjects if this behavior isn't addressed.

Mrs. Woolsey, Canton Elementary School, 3rd grade

Mrs. Woolsey's note perfectly summed up my childhood. She addressed it, "To Whom It May Concern" because she had no idea who would take on the responsibility for dealing with my "disruptive behavior". Then she assumed there would be someone who cared about me enough to talk to me about her concerns, when, in fact, there was no one. What my 3rd grade teacher was observing from the outside was the fact that I was encapsulated in my bubble on the inside. She was right.

I was totally oblivious to the world around me. It was deliberate. No amount of adult criticism would have had any effect on me. I was inside my safe zone and I wasn't going to engage the world unless I absolutely had to. She was also right that I was constantly on the receiving end of some pretty vicious bullying. However, she was wrong when she wrote that I had no reaction to it. I cared deeply. But my response was to burrow deeper inside my make-believe world, so that there would be no pain.

I did find a way to balance my love for academia with my need for safety as I got a bit older. I had such a thirst for learning that I was willing to emerge from my bubble long enough to soak in as much information as I could. I read constantly and studied intensely. In 8th grade I won an all-expenses-paid scholarship to a summer college program for advanced middle school students. I lived on a college campus for an entire summer, with no caretakers, no trauma, and no terror. I made friends (okay, two friends) and studied college classes like human physiology and psychology. It was at this program that I decided I wanted to go to medical school and become a psychiatrist. I wanted to cure psychosis. I decided someone had to take on the disease that had ravaged my childhood. Suddenly, at 13 years old, I found myself with a goal and a plan for the future.

What I also discovered during that summer was that I didn't need my inner world so much when I wasn't mired in chaos. I wasn't self-aware enough to understand that my bubble was my cloak of protection. I could wear it if I needed it and hang it up when in safety. Nothing threatened me that summer in 1974 and I matured, without my cloak, in huge strides and in just a few months.

*

With faith in G-d and the intellect He blessed me with, I endured and survived a dark childhood. But I had no way of knowing, as I made my exodus from the Egypt that was my childhood into the desert of my adulthood, what a battle I would have to fight to reach the promised land of true emancipation.

I entered my young adulthood a tumbleweed, blowing from university to university, graduate school to graduate school, even flirting with a medical school admission, without ever finishing anything more than my bachelor's degree and a graduate school degree I never planned to finish.

My undergrad experience was tumultuous. I attended two colleges, one of which I was driven out of by campus gossip. I was assaulted in my dorm room by a young man with religious delusions. Just when I thought I would never again be the victim of someone else's psychosis, there I was – at 3am one morning in 1979 – face-to-face with an assailant who called me Jezebel and compared me to a Moabite woman.

My assault became fodder for campus rumormongering, and so I fled the blather factory for a religious school half-way across the country. The dorms had bed checks, curfews, and a ban on men. I felt sheltered, and from within that cocoon I finished my bachelor's degree in chemistry. I applied to medical school and received an invitation for an interview.

However, simultaneously, I was drowning in my first deep and profound bipolar depression. I was carried through my senior year by one of my chemistry professors and my rabbi. My medical school interview was a disaster. In the middle of being questioned, I burst into involuntary sobs and found myself rocking, with my head buried in my hands. I walked out, never completing the interview. I was humiliated. My descent into bipolar disorder destroyed my 8th grade dream of becoming a physician. I was now directionless.

I belonged nowhere, to no one, least of all to myself. I was 23 years old – with no human ties I would admit to – and facing a future I couldn't find a place in.

I tumbled into Chicago one year and took a job as a research assistant, taking grad classes at the same time. The job and classes held my attention long enough that I stayed in one spot for over a year. One day, as I puzzled out my future in the graduate student lounge, a poster caught my eye. It said, "Join the Peace Corps, Make a Difference in People's Lives, Change Your Own."

All the neurons in my brain fired simultaneously. This was my answer. This was a giant neon postcard and on it was my destiny. Eight months later, I was on a plane to East Africa with 70 other volunteers for a two-year commitment, with no clue as to what I had undertaken. All I knew was that 10,000 miles would separate me from Boston, my childhood residence. For the first time in 24 years, I could breathe.

But I was grossly ill-prepared; not for my work or the culture, but for the changes that would take place inside my own psyche. I joined the Peace Corps to flee my tangled past, but all I managed to do was bunch those threads into one big jumbled knot.

It started innocently enough. We were a group of Peace Corps volunteers, swapping stories about home while in training – for four months – to live and work in a complex and ancient culture. As I sat in one of the mud-walled training huts one day, listening to the group reminisce about childhood escapades, a panic swelled in my gut. What was I going to say?

Should I sit silent? Should I leave?

I was in mid-alarm. I had no time to flee; I was next in the circle. So, from somewhere deep inside my inner childhood world came a story about a family vacation that was idyllic, adventurous, and pulled straight from a Brady Bunch episode. I regaled everyone with a tale of a trip to the Grand Canyon when I was eight. I talked about taking a burro down to the base of the canyon and how my dad rode protectively by my side for the entire descent. I described the panoramic view, the exquisite rock formations, and the sound of the Colorado River splashing with almost the echo of a giggle.

My ruse worked. My "memory" was met with head nods and "wows". From that moment on, I reinvented where I came from and how I grew up, based on the adventures from my beloved childhood television programs. I couldn't verbalize the truth about my life, so fantasy became reality as a substitute. I had found a new way to escape.

Peace Corps had – and still has – a persnickety attitude toward volunteers staying in-country indefinitely, so I stayed as long as I could, which was for three years. My future husband, Joe, left a year earlier. Joe had been my nearest Peace Corps neighbor and we'd begun a romance in our very remote corner of the Rift Valley.

It was now my turn to leave the volatile but protective cocoon of Africa. I had to go back to the U.S., and that meant going back to Boston. I couldn't travel there and bring my television family memories with me. I needed those "memories" to be unchallenged so that I could draw on them again if I ever needed them. I grieved at the cruelty of having to say goodbye to all those comforting "reminiscences".

I did stop in one country on my way back to the States, though: Israel. I hung out in Jerusalem for six weeks. I was desperate to reconnect with the G-d who had shepherded me through the abyss of my childhood. In Peace Corps, by living a lie, I had traded my principles for the illusion of safety. That reality shamed me.

I needed redemption so I could reclaim my soul. I had lost it somewhere between tales of the Grand Canyon and a mother–daughter banquet.

There, at the Western Wall – just like with those Shabbos candles so long ago – G-d and I talked. I spent the next several evenings sobbing in my cot at the youth hostel. In the depth of my depression and shame, I was forced to cough up my ugly childhood memories like phlegm. Their return was a torment I didn't remember how to bear.

As my EL AL flight touched down in the U.S. in December of 1986, I instantly felt sick. Did I really have to go to Boston? But where else was I going to go?

I flew in and then flew back out days later, but this time I dragged more baggage with me than just my beat-up old duffle bag. Ultimately, I blew into Joe's backyard in the Midwest in January of 1987. I started yet another graduate school program, and Joe and I married in the fall of 1988 ...

Why not read these next?

Rattled

Overcoming Postpartum Psychosis

When Jen Wight gave birth to her son, she thought it was all uphill from there. But she was wrong. *Rattled* is the story of her journey through psychosis.

When the Bough Breaks

The Pursuit of Motherhood

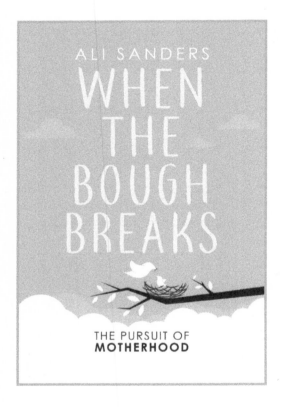

Motherhood was all Ali Sanders had
ever wanted out of life. She just didn't expect it to be
such a rocky road to happiness.

Depression in a Digital Age

The Highs and Lows of Perfectionism

Depression in a Digital Age traces the journey of a young woman's search for perfection in a world filled with filters.

the *Shaw* mind
FOUNDATION

Creating hope for children,
adults and families

Sign up to our charity, The Shaw Mind Foundation
www.shawmindfoundation.org
and keep in touch with us; we would love to hear
from you.

*We aim to bring to an end the suffering and despair caused
by mental health issues. Our goal is to make help and support
available for every single person in society, from all walks of
life. We will never stop offering hope. These are our promises.*

TRIGGER™
The mental health & wellbeing publisher

www.triggerpublishing.com

Trigger is a publishing house devoted to opening conversations about mental health. We tell the stories of people who have suffered from mental illnesses and recovered, so that others may learn from them.

Adam Shaw is a worldwide mental health advocate and philanthropist. Now in recovery from mental health issues, he is committed to helping others suffering from debilitating mental health issues through the global charity he co-founded, The Shaw Mind Foundation. www.shawmindfoundation.org

Lauren Callaghan (CPsychol, PGDipClinPsych, PgCert, MA (hons), LLB (hons), BA), born and educated in New Zealand, is an innovative industry-leading psychologist based in London, United Kingdom. Lauren has worked with children and young people, and their families, in a number of clinical settings providing evidence based treatments for a range of illnesses, including anxiety and obsessional problems. She was a psychologist at the specialist national treatment centres for severe obsessional problems in the UK and is renowned as an expert in the field of mental health, recognised for diagnosing and successfully treating OCD and anxiety related illnesses in particular. In addition to appearing as a treating clinician in the critically acclaimed and BAFTA award-winning documentary *Bedlam*, Lauren is a frequent guest speaker on mental health conditions in the media and at academic conferences. Lauren also acts as a guest lecturer and honorary researcher at the Institute of Psychiatry Kings College, UCL.

Find out more

www.triggerpublishing.com

You can find us everywhere @triggerpub